Higher
MODERN STUDIES

The Scottish Certificate of Education Examination Papers
are reprinted by special permission of
THE SCOTTISH QUALIFICATIONS AUTHORITY

ISBN 0 7169 9287 6
© *Robert Gibson & Sons, Glasgow, Ltd., 1998*

The publishers have wherever possible acknowledged the source of copyright material. They regret any inadvertent omission and will be pleased to make the necessary acknowledgement in future printings.

ROBERT GIBSON · Publisher
17 Fitzroy Place, Glasgow, G3 7SF.

SCOTTISH
CERTIFICATE OF
EDUCATION

Time: 2 hours 30 minutes

MODERN STUDIES
HIGHER GRADE
Paper I

INSTRUCTIONS TO CANDIDATES

Candidates should answer **four** questions—

One from Section A—Politics in a Democratic Society,

One from Section B—Income and Wealth in a Democratic Society and Health Care in a Democratic Society, and

Two from Section C—International Issues

The questions you answer in Section C must be chosen from different Study Themes. Within each Study Theme a choice of questions is provided.

Each question carries 25 marks.

Marks may be deducted for bad spelling and bad punctuation and for writing that is difficult to read.

CONTENTS

SCOTTISH
CERTIFICATE OF
EDUCATION
1993

MONDAY, 24 MAY
9.30 AM – 12.00 NOON

MODERN STUDIES
HIGHER GRADE
Paper I

SECTION A—Politics in a Democratic Society (Study Theme 1)
Answer ONE question from this Section

Marks

Question A1

(a) *"In recent years, the Labour Party has been accused of abandoning its socialist principles while the Conservative Party has been accused of abandoning Thatcherism."*

What policy changes made by each party have given rise to the claims in the statement above?   **13**

(b) Assess the success of other parties in mounting a challenge to the Conservative and Labour Parties in recent years.   **12**

   (25)

Question A2

(a) Examine the ways in which the mass media may influence voting behaviour in the UK.   **10**

(b) Discuss the other factors which may influence the way people vote.   **15**

   (25)

Question A3

"In our democracy it is right that Government Ministers, the Shadow Cabinet and backbench MPs are subject to a variety of pressures from outside Parliament. The danger for democracy is that some of those applying pressure are able to exert more influence than others."

(a) What are the pressures referred to in the quotation?   **15**

(b) Using examples, discuss the view that "the danger for democracy is that some of those applying pressure are able to exert more influence than others".   **10**

   (25)

Question A4

(a) Why is Proportional Representation (PR) considered by some people to be a fairer system, for both voters and political parties, than "first past the post"?   **13**

(b) Choose **two** systems of PR and, with specific reference to these two systems, discuss their **disadvantages**.   **12**

   (25)

Question A5

(a) To what extent has there been criticism of the way in which Scotland is governed?   **12**

(b) What are the attitudes of the political parties to suggested changes in the constitutional arrangements for Scotland?   **13**

   (25)

Question A6

(a) Describe the ways in which local authorities raise finance.   **5**

(b) In what ways has the raising of finance caused problems for local authorities in recent years?   **10**

(c) *"Party politics should play no part in local government."*

Discuss.   **10**

   (25)

SECTION B—Income and Wealth in a Democratic Society (Study Theme 2), Health Care in a Democratic Society (Study Theme 3)

Answer ONE question from this Section

Marks

Question B7

Study Reference Table QB7 and answer the questions below.

Reference Table QB7: UK Living Standards—Selected Indicators 1990

	South East	West Midlands	North West	Scotland
Average Weekly Earnings (£)	312	247	253	253
Unemployment	784,224	258,792	321,956	241,351
Expenditure on National Insurance Benefits (£ Millions)	11,581	3,551	4,897	3,786
Consumer Expenditure (£ per head)	7,126	5,610	5,719	5,606
Mortgage Advances	215,000	58,000	75,000	60,000

(a) Give reasons for the regional differences shown. **15**

(b) To what extent does Reference Table QB7 provide an incomplete picture of wealth **and** poverty in the UK? **10**

(25)

Question B8

(a) Examine the case for a national minimum wage in the UK. **15**

(b) **Other than a national minimum wage**, what policies, aimed at improving living standards, have caused disagreement between the Government and Opposition? **10**

(25)

Marks

Question B9

(a) Examine the view that racial disadvantage exists in the UK. **15**

(b) In what ways does race relations legislation attempt to eliminate racial disadvantage? **10**

(25)

Question B10

(a) What is meant by the term "Community Care"?

Why has the idea of Community Care received widespread support in recent years? **10**

(b) To what extent have recent Conservative Governments developed policies on Community Care for the elderly? **15**

(25)

Question B11

(a) In what ways have recent Conservative Governments encouraged a move towards competitive tendering in the Health Service? **10**

(b) Examine the arguments both for **and** against competitive tendering in the Health Service. **15**

(25)

Question B12

(a) What changes have recent Conservative Governments made to the way in which NHS hospitals are run? **10**

(b) Examine the criticisms which have been made of these changes. **15**

(25)

SECTION C—International Issues

Answer TWO questions from this Section

Please note that within each Study Theme a choice is provided.

Answer only ONE question in relation to a single Study Theme.

> **Throughout this Section, the terms "Soviet Union" and "Soviet" refer to the Republics which made up the Soviet Union until 1991.**

REGIONAL AND NATIONAL CONFLICT (STUDY THEME 4)

Marks

Question C13

EITHER A   South Africa

A.   (*a*)   To what extent has there been constitutional change in South Africa in recent years?   **13**

(*b*)   In what ways has the social and economic situation of **both** white and non-white South Africans altered in recent years?   **12**

(25)

OR B   Arab-Israeli Conflict

B.   (*a*)   Discuss the continuing social and economic problems faced by Palestinians throughout the Middle East.   **13**

(*b*)   Examine the main obstacles to lasting peace in the Middle East.   **12**

(25)

MINORITIES (STUDY THEME 5)

Question C14

EITHER A   National and Religious Minorities in the Soviet Union

A.   (*a*)   In what ways did the religious and national minorities in the Soviet Union take advantage of Gorbachev's policy of "glasnost"?   **15**

(*b*)   To what extent was national identity linked to religious identity?   **10**

(25)

OR B   Ethnic Minorities in the USA

B.   (*a*)   In which areas of the USA are the populations of African Americans (Blacks) and Hispanics most heavily concentrated?

Why are they concentrated in these areas?   **10**

(*b*)   Examine the social, economic and political problems which are to be found in areas which have large population concentrations of both African Americans and Hispanics.   **15**

(25)

INTERNATIONAL COOPERATION AND CONFLICT (STUDY THEME 6)

Marks

Question C15

EITHER A   The European Community

A.   (*a*)   Discuss the part played by **each** of the following in the European Community:

the European Parliament;

the Commission;

the Council of Ministers.   **10**

Answer either part (b) or part (c)

(*b*)   (i)   Describe the main features **and** benefits of the regional policy of the EC.   **8**

(ii)   Discuss the difficulties involved in putting the policy into practice.   **7**

or

(*c*)   (i)   What is meant by the "harmonisation of markets"?   **7**

(ii)   To what extent has the harmonisation of markets caused difficulties for the UK?   **8**

(25)

OR B   The USA and the Soviet Union

B.   (*a*)   In what ways did the USA **and** the Soviet Union promote their interests in Central America **and** the Persian Gulf?   **15**

(*b*)   What evidence is there of continuing US influence in **either** Central America **or** the Persian Gulf?   **10**

(25)

IDEOLOGY AND DEVELOPMENTS (STUDY THEME 7)

Question C16

EITHER A   The USA

A.   (*a*)   Describe the ways in which State and Federal authorities attempt to regulate economic activity in the USA.   **12**

(*b*)   *"New technology and the changing distribution of jobs are having devastating effects on low-skilled workers and women in the USA."*

Discuss.   **13**

(25)

OR B   The Soviet Union

B.   (*a*)   Discuss the social, economic and political effects of Communist ideology on the citizens of the Soviet Union.   **15**

(*b*)   Why did Mr Gorbachev's policies for reconstructing the Soviet economy fail?   **10**

(25)

OR C   China

C.   (*a*)   Examine the social and economic consequences for Chinese citizens of the shift from Maoism in recent years.   **15**

(*b*)   What has been the reaction of the Chinese authorities to demands for political change?   **10**

(25)

POLITICS OF THE ENVIRONMENT (STUDY THEME 8)

Marks

Question C17

    EITHER A   The Politics of Energy

A.   (*a*)   What are the economic and environmental effects of the exploitation of different forms of energy?   **15**

        (*b*)   Examine the effectiveness of pressure groups in influencing policies on nuclear energy in **one** of the following countries:

            UK;

            Germany;

            USA.   **10**

            (25)

    OR B   The Politics of Food

B.   **With reference to either North East Africa (excluding Egypt) or Southern Africa, answer the questions below.**

        (*a*)   Choose **three** of the following and explain why they have caused food shortages.

            Domestic political problems

            War

            Debt

            Dependence on primary products

            Land ownership

            Cash crop production   **15**

        (*b*)   Examine the effectiveness of aid from international agencies, governments and voluntary organisations.   **10**

            (25)

[END OF QUESTION PAPER]

SCOTTISH
CERTIFICATE OF
EDUCATION
1994

WEDNESDAY, 25 MAY
9.30 AM – 12.00 NOON

MODERN STUDIES
HIGHER GRADE
Paper I

SECTION A—Politics in a Democratic Society (Study Theme 1)

Answer ONE question from this Section

Marks

Question A1

(a) Discuss the main influences on policy making on the Labour and Conservative Parties. **13**

(b) Compare Labour and Conservative policies on:

education;

public and private ownership. **12**

(25)

Question A2

"The conflicting demands of the constituency, national interest, the Parliamentary party, pressure group interest, personal conscience make the role of an MP in our democracy impossible."

(a) Describe the work of a backbench MP both inside and outside Parliament. **12**

(b) Examine the view expressed in the above statement. **13**

(25)

Question A3

"The powers of the Prime Minister can be controlled in the Cabinet and in Parliament. However, the extent to which these powers can be controlled depends on the style of leadership and the personality of the Prime Minister."

(a) Describe the powers of the Prime Minister. **12**

(b) Examine the view expressed in the above statement. **13**

(25)

Question A4

(a) Describe the part played by senior Civil Servants in the UK political system. **10**

(b) Examine the ways in which pressure groups attempt to influence political decisions in the UK. **15**

(25)

Question A5

(a) What are the functions of the Secretary of State for Scotland, the Scottish Office and Parliament in the government of Scotland? **15**

(b) Discuss recent proposals for reforming the way in which Scotland is governed. **10**

(25)

Question A6

(a) Why does the Government believe that the reform of local government is necessary? **10**

(b) Discuss the proposed reforms of local government in Scotland. **15**

(25)

**SECTION B—Income and Wealth in a Democratic Society (Study Theme 2),
Health Care in a Democratic Society (Study Theme 3)**

Answer ONE question from this Section

Marks

Question B7

(a) Describe the ways in which social class can be defined.   **12**

(b) What evidence is there of continued social and economic inequality between social classes in
the UK?   **13**

(25)

Question B8

Study Reference Table QB8 and answer the questions below.

Reference Table QB8: Mean Gross Weekly Earnings for Selected Occupations in the UK.

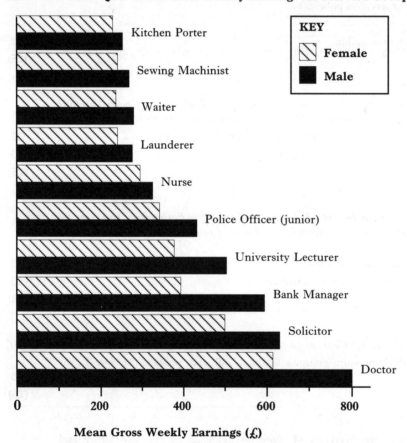

Source: New Earnings Survey 1992

(a) Discuss the differences between male and female earnings in the UK.   **12**

(b) To what extent are women making political progress in the UK?   **13**

(25)

Marks

Question B9

(*a*) Examine the main causes of unemployment.   **10**

(*b*) In what ways have recent Governments tried to create employment?
       What criticisms have been made of these attempts?   **15**

                                                                                    (25)

Question B10

(*a*) What policies have Governments introduced to improve patient care in National Health
       Service hospitals in recent years?   **15**

(*b*) Examine the criticisms which have been made of these policies.   **10**

                                                                                    (25)

Question B11

(*a*) What evidence is there of inequalities in health in the UK?
       Give reasons for these inequalities in health.   **15**

(*b*) Examine the role of preventative medicine and positive health care campaigns in improving
       the health of the nation.   **10**

                                                                                    (25)

Question B12

(*a*) In what ways do **each** of the following organise their efforts to influence health care policy?

           Employees
           Consumers
           Commercial groups   **12**

(*b*) Examine the issues which have caused conflict between the Government and employees in
       the health care industry in recent years.   **13**

                                                                                    (25)

SECTION C—International Issues

Answer TWO questions from this Section

Please note that within each Study Theme a choice is provided.

Answer only ONE question in relation to a single Study Theme.

REGIONAL AND NATIONAL CONFLICT (STUDY THEME 4)

Marks

Question C13

EITHER A   South Africa

A. (*a*) Why was South Africa condemned by the international community for so many years? **10**

    (*b*) Discuss the economic and social progress made by the people of South Africa since the dismantling of apartheid. **15**

(25)

OR B   Arab-Israeli Conflict

B. (*a*) In what ways have the Palestinian people attempted to promote their cause in recent years? **9**

    (*b*) Examine the Israeli response **both** to the Palestinian cause **and** to the methods used to promote it in recent years. **9**

    (*c*) What political divisions **within** Israel hinder progress towards reform? **7**

(25)

MINORITIES (STUDY THEME 5)

Question C14

EITHER A   National and Religious Minorities in the Soviet Union and its Successor States

A. (*a*) Describe the treatment of religion and religious groups in the former Soviet Union. **12**

    (*b*) What evidence is there of a revival of religion and nationalism in the successor states of the Soviet Union? **13**

OR B   Ethnic Minorities in the USA **(25)**

B. *"Despite advances in political representation made by minority groups, they continue to experience social and economic disadvantages."*

    (*a*) To what extent have minority groups made political progess in the USA in recent years? **10**

    (*b*) What evidence is there that minority groups continue to experience social and economic disadvantages? **15**

(25)

INTERNATIONAL COOPERATION AND CONFLICT (STUDY THEME 6)

Marks

Question C15

EITHER A   The European Community

A.   (*a*) Why have recent attempts at closer co-operation within the EC caused problems for some of the member states?   **13**

(*b*) Examine the advantages and disadvantages for the EC of increased membership.   **12**

(25)

OR B   The United Nations

B.   Study Reference Map QC15B and answer the questions below.

Reference Map QC15B

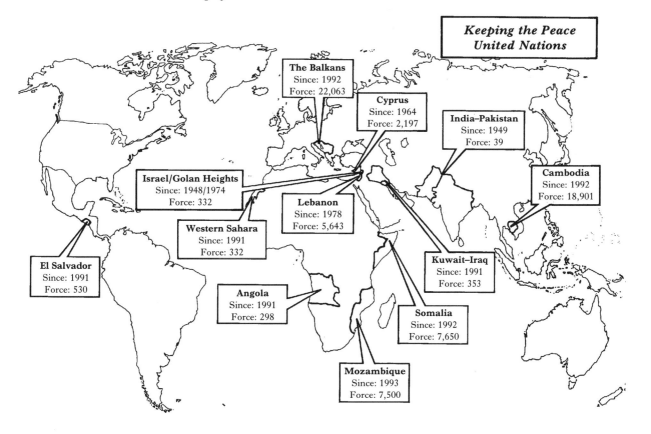

(*a*) What are the main aims of the United Nations Organisation?   **5**

(*b*) What methods may be used by the United Nations in its peacekeeping role to intervene in disputes between members?   **10**

(*c*) **Using recent examples**, assess how successful the United Nations has been in solving disputes.   **10**

(25)

IDEOLOGY AND DEVELOPMENT (STUDY THEME 7)

Marks

Question C16

EITHER A   The USA

A. (a) What are the main problems faced by the United States economy?   **12**

   (b) In what ways have recent administrations attempted to solve these problems?

      How successful have they been?   **13**

      (25)

OR B   Russia

B. (a) Assess the economic effects which central planning had on industry and agriculture in the former Soviet Union.   **8**

   (b) What are the main problems now facing industry and agriculture in Russia?   **8**

   (c) Examine the social problems which have arisen as a result of recent ideological changes in Russia.   **9**

      (25)

OR C   China

C. (a) To what extent has there been progress in the Chinese economy in recent years?   **15**

   (b) Discuss the social problems which have faced China in recent years.   **10**

      (25)

POLITICS OF THE ENVIRONMENT (STUDY THEME 8)

Question C17

EITHER A   The Politics of Energy

A. (a) What criticisms are there of the British Government's energy policy?   **12**

   (b) Assess the environmental effects of the exploitation of various forms of energy.   **13**

      (25)

OR B   The Politics of Food

B. **With reference to either North East Africa (excluding Egypt) or Southern Africa, answer the questions below.**

   (a) Assess the effectiveness of the responses of both international and voluntary organisations to food shortages.   **13**

   (b) Why do countries give bi-lateral aid?

      What are the criticisms of this type of aid?   **12**

      (25)

[END OF QUESTION PAPER]

SCOTTISH
CERTIFICATE OF
EDUCATION
1994

WEDNESDAY, 25 MAY
1.30 PM – 4.00 PM

MODERN STUDIES
HIGHER GRADE
Paper II
Decision Making Exercise 1

Attempt:

EITHER   Decision Making Exercise 1: Income and Wealth in a Democratic Society

OR   Decision Making Exercise 2: Health Care in a Democratic Society but <u>not both</u>. The Decision Making Exercises are contained in separate booklets.

A summary of the exercise is provided on the cover of each booklet.

Read the summaries carefully before deciding which exercise to attempt. In each case, answer ALL questions.

DECISION MAKING EXERCISE 1 :

INCOME AND WEALTH IN A DEMOCRATIC SOCIETY

Summary of Decision Making Exercise

You are a researcher employed by the Forthside Regional Council.

Prepare a report for submission to the Council recommending or rejecting the setting up of an Unemployment Resources Centre in the city of Northglen which is in Forthside Region (Question 5).

Before beginning the task, you must answer a number of evaluating questions (Questions 1–4) based on the source material provided. The source material is as follows:

SOURCE A: Statement by Charles Murray

SOURCE B: Newspaper Article

SOURCE C: Statistical Survey

SOURCE D: Letters to the Northglen Advertiser

DECISION MAKING EXERCISE 1

QUESTIONS

Marks

Questions 1 to 4 are based on the Sources A to D on pages 2—6.   Answer Questions 1 to 4 before attempting Question 5.

In Questions 1 to 4, use <u>only</u> the sources described in each question.

Question 1

*Use **only** Source A and Source C1.*

Give evidence to support and counter Charles Murray's claims on spending by the Government.

3

Question 2

(*a*) *Use **only** Source A and Source B.*

Examine the differing views of Charles Murray and the Newspaper Article on "people's attitude to work".

2

(*b*) *Use **only** Source A and Source C2.*

To what extent does the data in Table C2 support Charles Murray's views on single parent families (Source A, lines 16—20)?

2

Question 3

*Use **only** Source A, Source B and Source C4.*

Give arguments against the view on consumer spending expressed by Charles Murray in the last paragraph of Source A.

3

Question 4

(*a*) *Use **only** Source C3, Source D1 and Source D2.*

In what way could the information given in Source C3 be used by both Susan Taylor and Councillor Ross to back-up their view on benefits?

2

(*b*) *Use **only** Source C5 and Source D2.*

Quote an example of exaggeration from Source D2. Give reasons for your choice.

3

(15)

Marks

Question 5

DECISION MAKING TASK

You are a researcher employed by Forthside Regional Council and are asked to prepare a report recommending or rejecting the setting up of an Unemployment Resources Centre in the city of Northglen.

In your report you should:
* recommend whether or not the Regional Council should establish and fund an Unemployment Resources Centre;
* provide arguments to support your recommendations, giving reasons why you rejected other options;
* describe any difficulties or cost implications which might follow from your recommendations.

In your report you **must** use:
* the **source material** provided and
* other **background knowledge**.

Your answer should be written in a style appropriate to a *report*.

The written and statistical information sources which have been provided are as follows:

SOURCE A: Statement by Charles Murray

SOURCE B: Newspaper Article

SOURCE C: Statistical Survey

SOURCE D: Letters to the Northglen Advertiser

(35)

Total: 50 Marks

SOURCE A: STATEMENT BY CHARLES MURRAY

The poor have built their own barriers. An underclass has developed because the old values of personal responsibility and self-discipline have been abandoned. The two-parent family has broken down due to a lack of morality and alongside this the willingness to work has disappeared. This has caused
5 poverty.

State benefits have only encouraged this trend. All they do is encourage the lazy. Furthermore, the Unemployment Resources Centres that we see springing up in left-wing controlled local authorities are funded by local authority grants and often expect to get their premises rent and rate free.

10 These Unemployment Resources Centres state that their function is to give advice on how to get as much as possible out of the welfare system and all of this at council taxpayers' expense! But this information is freely and easily available from the Department of Social Security so the state is providing this information already. What is more sinister is that often these centres are the
15 pet project of political activists and so become a focus for discontent.

The growth in the number of single parent families continues at an alarming rate and this has meant that the bulk of the money, both nationally and locally, is being wasted by them. They are the biggest drain on our system. Spending on social security has nearly doubled, both in monetary terms and
20 as a proportion of Government expenditure since 1981. Single parent families deprive children of positive male role models and reflect the decline of moral values. The Government should lead the fight against this moral decay by cutting benefits to lone mothers and diverting these funds to adoption agencies and orphanages. Single parent families are an underclass because
25 they will not work or conform to the norms of society.

If we see the poor as those in society who have least, then we will always have poverty. But Scotland is not like some poor Third World country. We do not have starvation and everyone has enough to eat. Very often people are poor due to their greed for consumer goods. They want what they cannot afford,
30 spending their money on satellite dishes and Reebok trainers.

Source: Adapted from *The Scotsman*, 4 June 1992

SOURCE B: ARTICLE FROM THE NORTHGLEN ADVERTISER

Britain is seeing the growth of an underclass. Generations are cut off from the world of work, living on the margins. This creates a new poverty. We now have a pool of unskilled labour. Many youngsters would love to learn a trade but there are few apprenticeships now and too few good training places.

5 People do want to work but unemployment tends to be concentrated in families because many jobs are obtained not by what you know but rather who you know. Some people are being turned down for interviews because of their address. Unemployment to many is now a way of life. There are children leaving school whose parents have not worked for years. The more children
10 you have the greater your chances of being poor.

An Unemployment Resources Centre can provide a range of support services such as information provision, a drop-in centre for mutual support. It can organise pressure group activity to get privileges for the unemployed. Where you live also contributes to poverty. Local shops are dearer than out of the
15 area hypermarkets—where a car is a necessity. Often houses are damp and therefore more expensive to heat. In housing schemes up and down the country you see people doing all sorts of things to get by: scavenging on skips; looking for things to use and sell. This is enterprise under difficult circumstances. In deprived schemes such as Northglen they patch-up, re-use,
20 make do and mend. The only shops booming in this recession, apart from pawn shops, are the charity shops. Best sellers are bedding, cooking pots and clothing—no arguing here over the labels on the trainers.

It is estimated that 75% of the population of Scotland use credit facilities but divisions occur—mortgages and credit cards for the wealthy, and pawn
25 brokers and money lenders for the poor. The number of poor people is increasing. In 1965 one in 25 children lived in families who relied on state benefits but by 1985 this figure was one in five.

Changes in the benefit system have not helped. Research has shown that two-thirds of claimants feel the changes have left them worse off. More than half
30 of those who have applied for a grant or loan from the Social Fund have been turned down. Targeting the needy means that those who receive benefits feel guilty because they have to turn to the state for help. Family Credit already subsidises low paying employers but humiliates those who receive it by means testing. It is estimated that only 51% of those entitled to claim do so because
35 of the shame involved. From 1993, a lone mother claiming Family Credit or Income Support can be asked for details of the child's father. Money will be cut if she refuses to co-operate. Many separated and divorced women, however, receive no maintenance nor wish to be financially dependent on a man now effectively out of their lives.

Table C1: Government Expenditure on Social Security 1981—1989

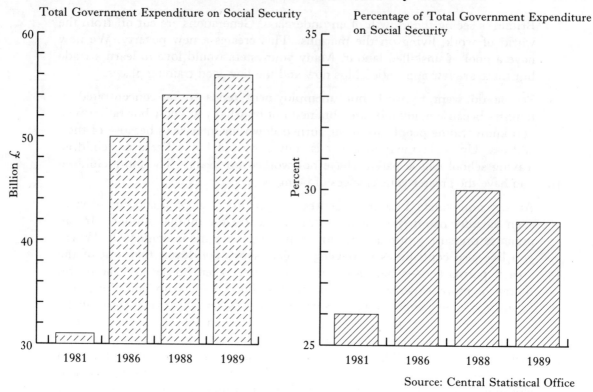

Total Government Expenditure on Social Security

Percentage of Total Government Expenditure on Social Security

Source: Central Statistical Office

Table C2: One Parent Families UK and Forthside Region

One Parent Families—% of all Households with Children in Forthside Region

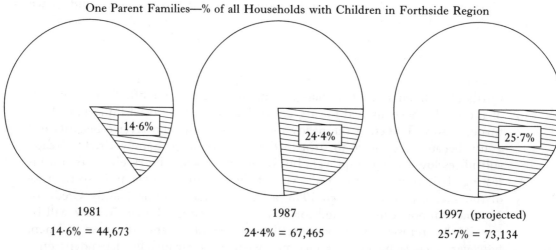

1981	1987	1997 (projected)
14·6% = 44,673	24·4% = 67,465	25·7% = 73,134

One Parent Families—At or Below
Supplementary Benefit Level in Forthside Region

Year	Could Claim	Did Claim
1987	45,906	41,775

Source: Department of Social Security

Total Government Spending on
One Parent Families in the UK

Year	Millions
1981-2	76
1987-8	163
1991-2	277

Table C3: Social Fund Expenditure in Forthside 1986—1991

	1986—1987 £m	1988—1989 £m	1989—1990 £m	1990—1991 £m
Single Payments	48·5	—	—	—
Social Fund				
Loans Budget	—	18·8	18·6	18·9
Grants Budget	—	8·0	7·6	7·6
Total Budget	—	26·8 %	26·2 %	26·5 %
Social Fund Budget as % of 1986/87 single payments (in "real terms")	—	51%	46%	43%

Table C4: Household Goods Owned in Forthside Region

% of Households With	Employed	Unemployed
Washing machines	93	77
Microwave Ovens	63	29
Dishwashers	18	4
Telephones	91	84
Televisions	99	98
Videos	81	36
Home Computers	29	5
CD Players	28	8

Table C5: Unemployment Benefit in Selected Countries of the EC (% of Average Earnings and Duration of Benefit)

Country	Earnings	Period of Benefit
Ireland	12%	6 months
Italy	20%	6 months
UK	14%	12 months
Belgium	60%	12 months
Luxembourg	80%	12 months
Denmark	90%	30 months

SOURCE D: LETTERS TO THE EDITOR OF THE NORTHGLEN ADVERTISER

Source D1

Sir—I must applaud this Government for taking positive steps and targeting benefits. Raising benefits across the board would just increase public spending— and this Government was elected to slash public spending. The social security reforms of 1988 were designed to target the needy and to reduce dependence on the
5 state. An example of this working well is the Social Fund where loans are given to people on low incomes who have special or emergency needs. These loans have to be paid back and so claimants now learn to budget. This Government has shown real determination to crack down on benefit fraud, making claimants prove that they have taken steps to find work before they are given any benefits. This means
10 they behave in a more socially acceptable manner and those who avoid their responsibility by not looking for work will feel the full force of the law.

Susan Taylor

Source D2

Sir—This Government's treatment of the poor is scandalous. They have slashed social security benefits—up until 1979 they rose in line with average earnings but, since then, they have only risen in line with prices and we are now lagging behind all the countries of the EC in unemployment benefits. The Social Fund involves
5 loans that have to be repaid and people being refused loans because they may not be able to repay them. If central government will not acknowledge poverty, then local government has to shoulder the responsibility. The Regional Council already gives free school meals, footwear and clothing grants to schoolchildren whose parents get Income Support. In 1979, 13% of the Region's population claimed Supplementary
10 Benefit, by 1987 it was 23% and in 1992, (despite changes in eligibility and threshold levels caused by the 1988 reforms) it stood at 20%. Reducing deprivation and disadvantage are the two priorities of this Regional Council. The Unemployment Resources Centres, already set up in other parts of regions, supply much needed advice on benefits and welfare rights and would be invaluable in an
15 area of multiple deprivation such as Northglen. The cost to the Region would be in the area of £25,000 a year: a small price to pay, bearing in mind we are applying for additional funding from the EC.

Councillor Andrew Ross

[END OF QUESTION PAPER]

SCOTTISH
CERTIFICATE OF
EDUCATION
1994

WEDNESDAY, 25 MAY
1.30 PM – 4.00 PM

MODERN STUDIES
HIGHER GRADE
Paper II
Decision Making Exercise 2

Attempt:

EITHER   Decision Making Exercise 1: Income and Wealth in a Democratic Society

OR   Decision Making Exercise 2: Health Care in a Democratic Society but <u>not both</u>. The Decision Making Exercises are contained in separate booklets.

A summary of the exercise is provided on the cover of each booklet.

Read the summaries carefully before deciding which exercise to attempt. In each case, answer ALL questions.

DECISION MAKING EXERCISE 2 :

HEALTH CARE IN A DEMOCRATIC SOCIETY

Summary of Decision Making Exercise

You are the Organising Secretary of the Fenwick Help the Aged Committee.

Prepare a report for submission to the Scottish Executive of Help the Aged which reviews the provision of health care for the elderly in Fenwick Region (Question 5).

Before beginning the task, you must answer a number of evaluating questions (Questions 1–4) based on the source material provided. The source material is as follows:

SOURCE A:	Newspaper Editorial
SOURCE B:	Statement by a "Scottish Action on Dementia" Spokesperson
SOURCE C:	Statistical Survey
SOURCE D:	Viewpoints

DECISION MAKING EXERCISE 2

QUESTIONS

Marks

Questions 1 to 4 are based on the Sources A to D on pages 2—6. Answer Questions 1 to 4 before attempting Question 5.

In Questions 1 to 4, use only the sources described in each question.

Question 1

(a) Use **only** *Source A and Source C1.*

Quote an example of exaggeration from Source A. Give reasons for your choice.   **3**

(b) Use **only** *Source A, Source C2 and Source C3.*

To what extent does the information in Sources C2 and C3 support the claim made in Source A about the creation of "a mixed economy of care"?   **2**

Question 2

Use **only** *Source B, Source C1 and Source C3.*

To what extent is Fenwick Health Board responding to the demand for services that are appropriate to the needs of old people with dementia?   **3**

Question 3

Use **only** *Source D1, Source D2 and Source C4.*

What evidence is there that **both** Anne Hood and John Burt have been selective in their use of facts when making statements about carers?   **4**

Question 4

Use **only** *Source D1 and Source D2.*

In what way **and** for what reason does the view of John Burt, on the responsibility for the care of the elderly, differ from that of Anne Hood?   **3**

(15)

Marks

Question 5

DECISION MAKING TASK

You are the Organising Secretary of the Fenwick Help the Aged Committee. Prepare a report for submission to the Scottish Executive of Help the Aged which reviews the provision of health care for the elderly in Fenwick Region.

In your report you should:

*   describe the community care policy for the elderly in Fenwick Region;
*   provide arguments for those parts of the policy with which you are in agreement;
*   identify and provide arguments for any changes you would welcome in this policy;
*   provide arguments which might be put forward by opponents to counter your suggestions.

In your report you **must** use:

*   the **source material** provided and
*   other **background knowledge**.

Your answer should be written in a style appropriate to a *report*.

The written and statistical information sources which have been provided are as follows:

SOURCE A: Newspaper Editorial

SOURCE B: Statement by a "Scottish Action on Dementia" Spokesperson

SOURCE C: Statistical Survey

SOURCE D: Viewpoints

(35)

Total: 50 Marks

SOURCE A: NEWSPAPER EDITORIAL

WHO CARES?

The huge growth in the numbers of old people in each of Fenwick Region's four Districts threatens to overwhelm health and social services. However, the problems of an ageing population are not unique to Fenwick. The Government, local authorities, health boards and voluntary organisations
5   agree that the ideal solution is to keep elderly people living independently at home for as long as possible with whatever support is necessary.

To achieve this, the Government has passed its Community Care Act. In broad terms a "mixed economy of care" has been created. Local authorities play a key role in making sure that care services are made available. Both
10   public and private organisations provide the care.

There are worries, however, that community care is simply a method of cutting back on public spending as the cost of caring for elderly people rises. The British Medical Association and the Association of Directors of Social Services have warned that community care is not a cheap option for meeting
15   the health and social needs of the elderly, disabled and vulnerable people in our society. They want more money to be available for Britain's carers.

Voluntary-sector organisations such as Age Concern, Mencap*, and others are worried about underfunding of community care. They fear that the Government has off-loaded responsibility for helping the sick and disabled
20   onto them.

At their most extreme, under-resourced community care programmes can lead to "granny dumping", as has happened in the USA. Elderly, infirm people have been left outside institutions by families that cannot afford to look after them. Studies of elderly people's families in this country by the Royal
25   Holloway and Bedford College, London, suggest that the concept of community care may be based on an out-of-date image of the family. Only one in four of those surveyed in the South Midlands had the type of extended family relationships that would be necessary for long term care outside a hospital or residential home.

30   Institutions like Marmion House, in Fenwick Region, which have provided long-stay places for the elderly, will close. Before this happens careful consideration must be given to where those people leaving them are going to live. It is not much fun coming out into the community if it means living in a cardboard box.

* Mental health organisation

Source: Adapted from *Education Guardian,* 12.5.92

SOURCE B: STATEMENT BY A "SCOTTISH ACTION ON DEMENTIA" SPOKESPERSON

If the elderly in general are considered vulnerable, the plight of those suffering from some degree of dementia has reached the proportions of a considerable crisis. We estimate that there are about 90,000 sufferers in Scotland, of whom almost 9,000 are in hospitals and another 3,000 in
5   residential homes. The rest, often looked after by carers who are just as physically frail, remain in the community. Here is a problem which calls for an urgent response. But that response is often provided by overstretched voluntary services.

Scotland has managed to get little right about community care for those with
10 dementia. There are few day care facilities. There is not anything like enough support for carers, many of whom are under tremendous personal stress. The demand for respite care is now so great that it is impossible to provide carers with the kind of break which allows them sufficient rest. Those with overall responsibility for community care should be looking to sub-contract this
15 service to voluntary agencies. They might also encourage use of the resource centre at Stirling University, which acts as an information exchange for all groups coping with dementia problems.

A crucial part of addressing the problem lies in early identification of the disease. Unfortunately some GPs delay making a diagnosis and, by the time a
20 person comes to our notice, he or she might have been suffering from the disease for as long as three years. Despite the distressing symptoms, there is no medical need for 90% of those suffering from dementia to be in hospital. Yet thousands of them are. Frequently, they are confined to long-stay mental hospitals where the accommodation takes the form of old and unsuitable
25 buildings located in remote areas. There can surely be no future for such places and they should be replaced at the earliest opportunity with services that are appropriate to the needs of old people with dementia. Hospital provision should consist of small-scale units which resemble, as closely as possible, domestic living conditions.

30 There is general agreement that we are facing a catastrophic epidemic. But because the misery lies behind closed doors, because the carers are too exhausted to organise support, because the voluntary agencies are overwhelmed and the public sector underfunded, it is a crisis too many people are content to keep secret.

SOURCE C: STATISTICAL SURVEY

Source C1
Map of Fenwick Region and Selected Statistical Information.

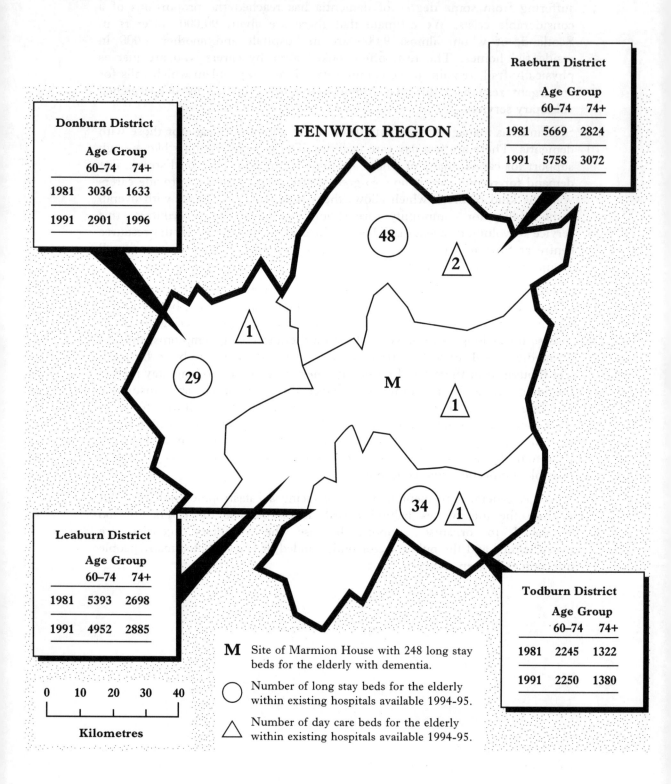

FENWICK REGION

Donburn District

	Age Group	
	60–74	74+
1981	3036	1633
1991	2901	1996

Raeburn District

	Age Group	
	60–74	74+
1981	5669	2824
1991	5758	3072

Leaburn District

	Age Group	
	60–74	74+
1981	5393	2698
1991	4952	2885

Todburn District

	Age Group	
	60–74	74+
1981	2245	1322
1991	2250	1380

M Site of Marmion House with 248 long stay beds for the elderly with dementia.

◯ Number of long stay beds for the elderly within existing hospitals available 1994-95.

△ Number of day care beds for the elderly within existing hospitals available 1994-95.

0   10   20   30   40

Kilometres

Source C2
Fenwick Health Board—Budget for Community Care (The Elderly) 1994-1995

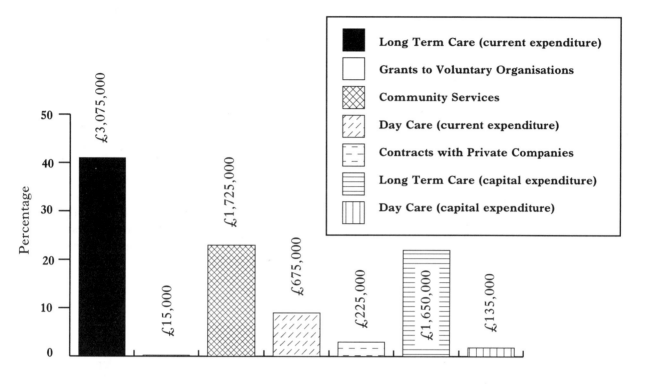

SOURCE C3
Fenwick Health Board
Proposed New Buildings
1994–95

Long-stay accommodation for elderly transferred out of Marmion House with dementia:

—25 bed unit in Leaburn.
—15 bed unit in Raeburn.
—10 bed unit in Donburn.
—25 bed unit in Todburn (jointly managed with private sector).

Day services for elderly:

—open day unit in Donburn with 10 places.

SOURCE C4
Fact File on Carers

Many dependent people are cared for by relatives or friends who provide their services free of charge. There are 6 million of these informal carers in the UK, 6 out of 10 of whom are women.

- THE CONSEQUENCES

- 57% of all carers who spend more than 20 hours a week caring for someone in the same house cannot take a break of 2 days; 8% of them find it very difficult to get away for even 2 hours.

- Half of all carers have long-standing health problems.

- One fifth of all carers look after more than one person.

- A quarter of them have been caring for someone for over 10 years.

SOURCE D: VIEWPOINTS

D1
VIEWPOINT OF ANNE HOOD

The state certainly has an obligation to the elderly, not least of which is to organise community resources to help the individual or the family provide the best care for those in need. I agree that the next generation of carers must be well informed about the allocation of home care assistants, meals on wheels and access to relief beds in
5 their area. However, most people acquire a moral code which is deep within us. Although I cannot stand in judgement of those who find it impossible, it is my belief that the family is ultimately responsible for the care of elderly members. In fact, I find that carers, particularly if they are close relatives, perform their duties because they want to. Carers report that looking after elderly relatives is a joy and none report
10 any ill-effects. The quality of life for the carer, with a little support from the state, can only be improved, not damaged, by sharing in the tasks of looking after others.

D2
VIEWPOINT OF JOHN BURT

The senile elderly can be terrifying, violent, dangerous and totally demanding. Massive help is needed to keep a 24-hour guard and that is precisely what is not available. The Government cries "do your duty" and most families obey with the burden always carried by a female member. Only very rich or self-sacrificing families
5 can give their senile old the full time care and devotion they need. Most people cannot manage it. With the divorce rate rising and, with the growth of the single parent family, there will soon be no chance of the continuation of this sweet little myth of every family doing its duty for its elderly. The population gets older, the problem gets bigger, but state provision for the elderly has steadily decreased. The
10 only increase is in the number of private homes for the elderly. The promise of care "from cradle to grave" is only kept for those who can pay. The state must accept full responsibility for the tender care of its senior citizens. It is for the state to legislate, not the family to suffer.

[END OF QUESTION PAPER]

SCOTTISH
CERTIFICATE OF
EDUCATION
1995

TUESDAY, 16 MAY
9.30 AM – 12.00 NOON

MODERN STUDIES
HIGHER GRADE
Paper I

SECTION A—Politics in a Democratic Society (Study Theme 1)

Answer ONE question from this Section

Question A1

Study Reference Table QA1 and answer the questions which follow.

Reference Table QA1: General Election Results 1974–1992

		Conservative	Labour	Liberal*	Others
February 1974	seats	296	301	14	24
	% vote	38	37	19	6
October 1974	seats	276	319	13	27
	% vote	36	39	18	7
1979	seats	339	268	11	17
	% vote	44	37	14	5
1983	seats	397	209	23	21
	% vote	42	28	25	5
1987	seats	376	229	22	23
	% vote	42	31	23	4
1992	seats	336	271	20	24
	% vote	42	34	18	6

* Liberal/SDP Alliance in 1983 and 1987; Liberal Democrat 1992.

Marks

(a) To what extent does a two party system exist in the UK?   12

(b) What internal party problems have faced the Labour Party and the Conservative Party?   13

    (25)

Question A2

(a) Examine the arguments **against** the "first past the post" electoral system in the UK.   12

(b) Describe factors affecting voting behaviour in the UK.   13

    (25)

Question A3

(a) Describe the role of the Cabinet Minister in the UK system of government.   12

(b) To what extent are the House of Commons and House of Lords able to control the actions of Governments?   13

    (25)

Question A4

    (*a*)   Describe, using examples, the different types of pressure groups in the UK.   **6**

    (*b*)   Outline the various methods used by pressure groups to influence government decisions.   **9**

    (*c*)   "*In recent years pressure groups have been unable to influence government decisions.*"

        Discuss.   **10**

        (25)

Question A5

    Examine the arguments for **and** against an increase in devolved power for Scotland.   **(25)**

Question A6

    (*a*)   "*Local authorities are not only providers of services but are also a necessary part of our democracy.*"

        Discuss.   **10**

    (*b*)   What criticisms have been made of the recent reforms of local government in Scotland?   **15**

        (25)

SECTION B—Income and Wealth in a Democratic Society (Study Theme 2), Health Care in a Democratic Society (Study Theme 3)

Answer ONE question from this Section

Question B7

    (*a*)   Examine the link between poverty and housing in the UK.   **12**

    (*b*)   **Other than housing**, describe those factors which can affect standards of living in the UK.   **13**

        (25)

Question B8

Study Reference Table QB8 and answer the questions which follow.

Reference Table QB8: Distribution of Household Income in the UK 1979–1989

	1979 %	1981 %	1987 %	1989 %
Top 1/5*	35·1	36·5	40·1	40·8
Next 1/5	23·1	23·1	22·9	23·3
Middle 1/5	18·1	17·8	17·1	17·0
Next 1/5	14·1	13·6	12·3	12·0
Bottom 1/5	9·6	9·0	7·6	6·9
	100·0	100·0	100·0	100·0

* Population divided into fifths.

Source: Social Trends 1993

    (*a*)   What evidence is there of an increasing gap between rich and poor in the UK?   **13**

    (*b*)   Compare Government and Opposition policies aimed at reducing poverty in the UK.   **12**

        (25)

Question B9

Study Reference Map QB9 and answer the questions which follow.

Reference Map QB9: UK Regional Unemployment

Average Regional Unemployment Rates for January 1993 are shown on Map.

% Increase since 1990

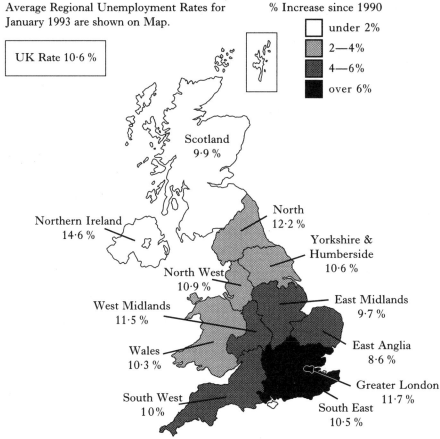

UK Rate 10·6 %

under 2%
2—4%
4—6%
over 6%

Scotland 9·9 %

North 12·2 %

Northern Ireland 14·6 %

Yorkshire & Humberside 10·6 %

North West 10·9 %

East Midlands 9·7 %

West Midlands 11·5 %

East Anglia 8·6 %

Wales 10·3 %

Greater London 11·7 %

South West 10%

South East 10·5 %

		Marks
(a)	Discuss the reasons for the trends in unemployment shown on the map.	**13**
(b)	What are the social effects of unemployment?	**12**
		(25)

Question B10

(a)	To what extent is the National Health Service meeting its original aims?	**13**
(b)	In what ways does the private sector contribute to health care in the UK?	**12**
		(25)

Question B11

(a)	What changes have been made in the provision of primary health care in the UK in recent years?	**13**
(b)	Examine the criticisms which have been made of these changes.	**12**
		(25)

Question B12

(a)	*"The Government has been forced to adopt new health care policies to cope with the increased proportion of elderly in the UK's population in recent years."*	
	Why has the proportion of the elderly in the UK's population increased in recent years?	**6**
(b)	What health care policies has the Government adopted to deal with the particular problems of the elderly?	**10**
(c)	Examine criticisms which have been made of these policies.	**9**
		(25)

SECTION C—International Issues

Answer TWO questions from this Section

Please note that within each Study Theme a choice is provided.

Answer only ONE question in relation to a single Study Theme.

REGIONAL AND NATIONAL CONFLICT (STUDY THEME 4)

Question C13   *Marks*

EITHER A   South Africa

A. (*a*) To what extent have black South Africans made social and economic progress since the dismantling of apartheid?   **15**

   (*b*) Describe the recent political changes in South Africa.   **10**
                                                                        (25)

OR B   Arab-Israeli Conflict

B. (*a*) To what extent has the international community been involved in seeking a solution to the Arab-Israeli conflict in recent years?   **13**

   (*b*) What obstacles remain to a lasting solution to the Arab-Israeli conflict?   **12**
                                                                        (25)

MINORITIES (STUDY THEME 5)

Question C14

EITHER A   National and Religious Minorities in the Soviet Union and its Successor States

A. (*a*) Describe the problems faced by minority groups in the successor states of the USSR.   **15**

   (*b*) Examine the progress made towards religious freedom in the successor states of the USSR.   **10**
                                                                        (25)

OR B   Ethnic Minorities in the USA

B. (*a*) Examine the success of measures taken by government to achieve social and economic equality for ethnic minorities in the USA.   **15**

   (*b*) Describe the ways in which ethnic minorities in the USA can help themselves to achieve economic, social and political equality.   **10**
                                                                        (25)

INTERNATIONAL COOPERATION AND CONFLICT (STUDY THEME 6)

Question C15

EITHER A   The European Community

A. (*a*) Outline the main aims of the European Union*.   **5**

   (*b*) Examine the contribution of the European Parliament and the Commission to the policies of the European Union.   **10**

   (*c*) What have been the main causes of disputes between member countries of the European Union in recent years?   **10**

   * the former European Community   **(25)**

OR B   The United Nations

B. (*a*) What are the roles of the General Assembly and the Security Council of the United Nations in contributing to world peace?   **13**

   (*b*) **With reference to two areas of conflict**, examine the success of the peacekeeping role of the UN in recent years.   **12**
                                                                        (25)

IDEOLOGY AND DEVELOPMENT (STUDY THEME 7)

Marks

Question C16

EITHER A   The USA

A. (*a*) What are the main features of the US market economy?   · **12**

    (*b*) To what extent do the Democrat Party and Republican Party differ in their economic policies?   **13**

                                                              (25)

OR B   Russia

B. (*a*) "*The Marxist-Leninist system no longer influences economic and social policy in Russia but the problems associated with it remain.*"

        Discuss.   **12**

    (*b*) Describe the political problems faced by the Russian leadership in recent years.   **13**

                                                              (25)

OR C   China

C. (*a*) To what extent has China moved towards a market economy in recent years?   **12**

    (*b*) Describe the political problems which have confronted the leaders of the Chinese Communist Party in recent years.   **13**

                                                              (25)

POLITICS OF THE ENVIRONMENT (STUDY THEME 8)

Question C17

EITHER A   The Politics of Energy

A. Examine the social, economic, environmental and political arguments concerning the development and use of nuclear energy.   **(25)**

OR B   The Politics of Food

B. **With reference to either North East Africa (excluding Egypt) or Southern Africa, answer the questions below.**

    (*a*) Choose **two** of the following and say why they have caused food shortages:

        land tenure;

        war;

        debt.   **13**

    (*b*) Examine the effectiveness of the work of the UN specialised agencies in responding to food shortages.   **12**

                                                                 (25)

[END OF QUESTION PAPER]

SCOTTISH
CERTIFICATE OF
EDUCATION
1995

TUESDAY, 16 MAY
1.30 PM – 4.00 PM

MODERN STUDIES
HIGHER GRADE
Paper II
Decision Making Exercise 1

Attempt:

Either   Decision Making Exercise 1: Income and Wealth in a Democratic Society;

Or   Decision Making Exercise 2: Health Care in a Democratic Society but **not both**. The Decision making Exercises are contained in separate booklets.

A summary of the exercise is provided on the cover of each booklet.

Read the summaries carefully before deciding which exercise to attempt. In each case, answer **all** questions.

DECISION MAKING EXERCISE 1 :

INCOME AND WEALTH IN A DEMOCRATIC SOCIETY

Summary of Decision Making Exercise

You are the Chairperson of Inverdee Region's Community Relations Sub-Committee. You have been asked by the Council to produce a paper arguing for or against positive discrimination in the recruitment and promotion of ethnic minorities in regional employment. (Question 5)

Before beginning the task, you must answer a number of evaluating questions (Questions 1–4) based on the source material provided. The source material is as follows:

SOURCE A: Extract from an Inverdee Council Policy Document

SOURCE B: Newspaper Article—Extract from Inverdee Argus

SOURCE C: Viewpoints

SOURCE D: Statistical Survey

DECISION MAKING EXERCISE 1

QUESTIONS

Marks

Questions 1 to 4 are based on Sources A to D on pages 2—7. Answer Questions 1 to 4 before attempting Question 5.

In Questions 1 to 4, use <u>only</u> the sources described in each question.

Question 1

(*a*) *Use* **only** *Source A and Source B.*

What differing views on racism in Scotland are expressed in Sources A and B?   **2**

(*b*) *Use* **only** *Source A, Source C2 and Source D1.*

Give evidence to support the different interpretations of Mohanjit Singh and Inverdee Regional Council on reported racial incidents.   **3**

Question 2

(*a*) *Use* **only** *Source B, Source C1 and Sources D3(a), D3(b) and D3(c).*

Using Sources D3(*a*), D3(*b*) and D3(*c*), compare the views of the newspaper article and Dorothy Thomas with relation to ethnic employment.   **4**

(*b*) *Use* **only** *Source B and Source D2.*

To what extent do the figures in Source D2 support the claim on the employment of ethnic minorities in local and central government?   **2**

Question 3

Use **only** *Source C1 and Source D4.*

To what extent could Dorothy Thomas be accused of being selective in her use of facts?   **2**

Question 4

Use **only** *Source C2 and Source D5.*

Quote an example of exaggeration by Mohanjit Singh. Give a reason for your choice.   **2**

(15)

Question 5

DECISION MAKING TASK

You are Chairperson of Inverdee Region's Community Relations Sub-committee. You have been asked by the Council to produce a paper arguing for or against positive discrimination in the recruitment and promotion of ethnic minorities in regional employment.

In your report you should:
* recommend whether or not Inverdee Regional Council should adopt the policy of positive discrimination in recruitment of employees;
* provide arguments to support your findings, giving reasons why you rejected the other option;
* describe any problems or difficulties which might follow from your findings.

In your report you **must** use:
* the **source material** provided and
* other **background knowledge**.

Your answer should be written in a style appropriate to a *report*.

The written and statistical information sources which have been provided are as follows:

SOURCE A: Extract from an Inverdee Council Policy Document

SOURCE B: Newspaper Article—Extract from Inverdee Argus

SOURCE C: Viewpoints

SOURCE D: Statistical Survey

(35)

Total: 50 Marks

SOURCE A: EXTRACT FROM AN INVERDEE COUNCIL POLICY DOCUMENT

Racism is not a problem in Scotland. Scotland has a good reputation for tolerance and this is borne out by the numbers from ethnic minorities who choose to live here.

Inverdee Regional Council is deeply committed to the task of ensuring
5 equality, justice and tolerance for all the people of Inverdee. The Council's policies are obviously succeeding as there have been no major outbreaks of racial unrest in the Region despite having one of the largest concentrations of ethnic minorities in Scotland. The number of reported racial incidents in the Region has increased, showing that people are now more aware of the steps
10 they can take to tackle racial abuse.

To further this policy, the Region has a Regional Community Relations Council (R.C.R.C.) jointly funded by the Regional Council and the Commission for Racial Equality. Its main job is to advise and help people who are subjected to racial harassment or who are having difficulties dealing
15 with statutory agencies in areas such as police, social work, health and housing.

The R.C.R.C. also provides an interpreting service—translating Regional documents into Punjabi, Bengali, Hindi, Gujerati, Urdu, and Chinese. In addition it provides oral translations for courts, police, housing, health, social
20 work, environmental health and social security meetings.

Several years ago, the Region held a "Multi-Racial Action Year" highlighting the benefits of living in an area that is home to a large proportion of the country's ethnic minorities. This included film nights, talks, festivals, art competitions and children's events, illustrating the range of cultural
25 backgrounds.

The Region's Education Department provides bi-lingual teaching, language schools for teaching English as a second language and multi-cultural education to build up respect and appreciation for different cultures. All education establishments in the Region have anti-racist policies. The ethnic minorities
30 in the Region enjoy a central place in our community.

SOURCE B: NEWSPAPER ARTICLE—EXTRACT FROM INVERDEE ARGUS

RACISM ON THE INCREASE

Racism is on the increase which shows that the Race Relations Act and the Regional Council's policies are failing. Nineteen years after the Act was passed to eliminate racial discrimination we find racism still alive and well in Scotland.

5 Ethnic families in housing schemes are subjected to racial harassment such as petrol or lighted matches being put through their letter boxes. Racial graffiti sprayed on shops, homes and cars is on the increase and many of these attacks are carried out by young children. In schools, racial taunts are making the lives of many youngsters miserable. The fact that there has been no major

10 outbreaks of racial unrest in Inverdee is more by good fortune than design.

The Inverdee Community Relations Council worries about racial discrimination in private house sales but public housing associations still do not recognise racial harassment as legitimate grounds for emergency rehousing.

15 Institutionalised racism is denying equal access to the job market for people from minorities. People of Asian origin have either been forced to become self-employed or take up the jobs rejected by the Scots—but even here promotion is rare.

Since 1976, there has been a Code of Practice for avoiding racial

20 discrimination in employment but this code does not have the force of law. It is obvious that recruitment and training of local and central government employees do not follow these codes for we do not employ enough people from the ethnic minorities. To redress the imbalance, we need positive discrimination. We need to re-think our policies to narrow our racial and

25 cultural differences, not accentuate them, as this Council does. Their policies divide people rather than uniting them.

What the Government and the Regional Council have to learn is that introducing preventative measures to combat discrimination and racism will not work on their own. The measures must be made to work and produce the

30 desired results. Monitoring and on-going reviews are time consuming and toothless. We need deterrents and real punishment for those who ignore laws and proper implementation of anti-racist, anti-harassment and anti-discriminatory measures.

It is all very well re-educating employees in racial issues and employing

35 translators but what we should do is employ more bi-lingual staff and have positive discrimination in housing allocations and Regional employment.

SOURCE C: VIEWPOINTS

Source C1

Viewpoint of Dorothy Thomas

I am in danger of being accused of being racist but I feel that the policies of the Council are unbalanced. In the past 50 years only 50,000 people of non-European origins have made their homes in Scotland. Large parts of our Region have few ethnic minorities living there but we all have to
5   endure this Council's obsession with anti racist policies. The Council has squandered £30,000 on a "Multi-Racial Action Year"—money that could have been put to better use to help all the people—not just a few!

Employers are now frightened of the power of the Industrial Tribunals in Racial Discrimination cases and so ethnic minorities have an unfair
10   advantage in applying for jobs with Scottish workers being passed over. The Council seems to be able to allocate houses to ethnic minorities while many Scots have to remain on waiting lists.

Source C2

Viewpoint of Mohanjit Singh

We are faced with racial abuse daily. The number of racial incidents is increasing every year and those reported are just the tip of the iceberg. Regional policies are failing. What is the point of reporting these incidents when the punishments are so pathetic?

5   The only way for the ethnic minorities to secure a proper place in the community is through politics. We need to stand and be selected as candidates and win seats in local government and Parliament. Only by doing this will we have the power to influence legislation and make changes. After all, white politicians only look after themselves and cannot
10   understand our problems. Regrettably there is no evidence so far of the ethnic minorities participating in politics at any level. Remember we are a powerful voting lobby. Punjabi is the second most spoken language in Scotland after English.

SOURCE D: STATISTICAL SURVEY

Table D1: Numbers of Reported Racial Incidents 1990–1992

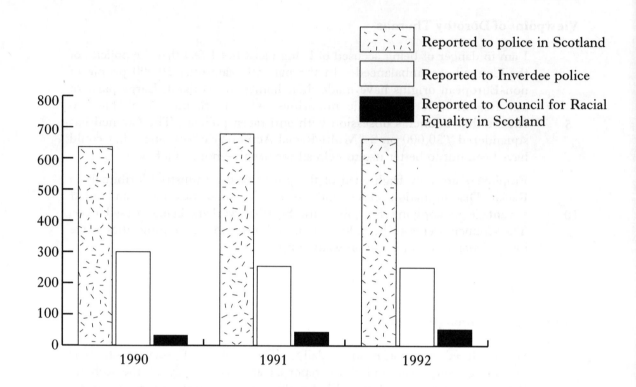

Table D2: Ethnic Population—Selected Employment 1993

	White	Ethnic	
Population of Scotland	4,934,610	63,957	(1·3%)
Population of Inverdee	2,212,727	35,979	(1·6%)
Staff employed by the Scottish Office	6,371	35	(0·5%)
Staff employed by Inverdee Council	100,350	725	(0·7%)
Inverdee—Selected Employment			
Administrative, Professional, Clerical & Technical	31,719	225	(0·7%)
Manual	34,945	132	(0·3%)
Teachers	25,329	354	(1·4%)
Police	6,801	13	(0·2%)
Fire	2,281	1	(0·04%)

Table D3(a): Breakdown of Ethnic Minorities in Scotland 1993

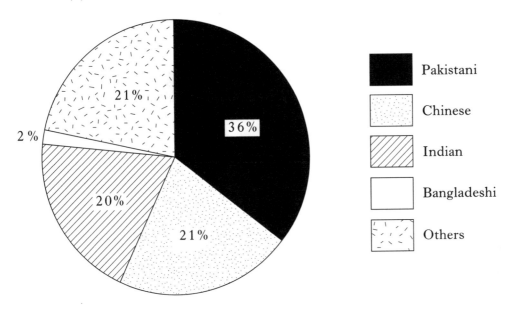

Legend:
- Pakistani (black)
- Chinese
- Indian
- Bangladeshi
- Others

Pie chart: 36% Pakistani, 21% (lower right), 20% Indian, 2%, 21% Others

Table D3(b): Scottish Unemployment 1991

Ethnic Group	Male	Female
White	14%	10%
Indian	18%	21%
Pakistani	24%	28%
Bangladeshi	11%	4%
Chinese	9%	8%

Table D3(c): Self-employment by Ethnic Origin (1991 Census)

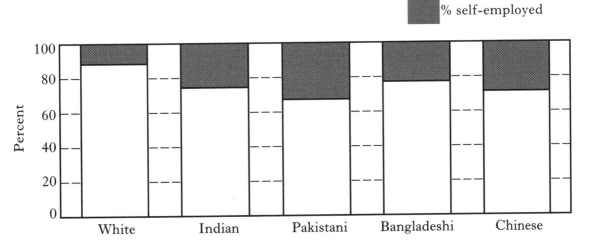

% self-employed

Table D4: Housing Tenure in Scotland

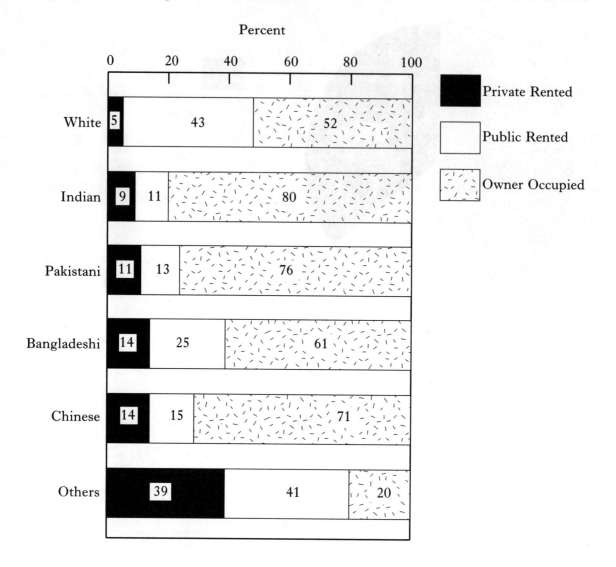

Percent

Private Rented
Public Rented
Owner Occupied

White	5	43	52
Indian	9	11	80
Pakistani	11	13	76
Bangladeshi	14	25	61
Chinese	14	15	71
Others	39	41	20

Table D5: Ethnic Minority Representation in Politics 1994

	White	*Ethnic*	*Total*
District Councillors in Scotland	1157	1	1158
Regional/Island Councillors in Scotland	522	2	524
Members in the House of Commons	645	6	651
Members in the House of Lords	1198	6	1204

[END OF QUESTION PAPER]

SCOTTISH
CERTIFICATE OF
EDUCATION
1995

TUESDAY, 16 MAY
1.30 PM – 4.00 PM

MODERN STUDIES
HIGHER GRADE
Paper II
Decision Making Exercise 2

Attempt:

Either   Decision Making Exercise 1:   Income and Wealth in a Democratic Society;

Or   Decision Making Exercise 2: Health Care in a Democratic Society but **not both**.
The Decision making Exercises are contained in separate booklets.

A summary of the exercise is provided on the cover of each booklet.

Read the summaries carefully before deciding which exercise to attempt. In each case, answer **all** questions.

DECISION MAKING EXERCISE 2:

HEALTH CARE IN A DEMOCRATIC SOCIETY

Summary of Decision Making Exercise

You are a civil servant from an overseas country on a fact finding visit to the Scottish Office. Your particular remit is health care. Prepare a report to send to your Government Minister of Health on the advisability of introducing an internal market into your own national system of state-funded health care (Question 5).

Before beginning the task, you must answer a number of evaluating questions (Questions 1–4) based on the source material provided. The source material is as follows:

Source A: Newspaper Editorial

Source B: Statement by a Health Union Spokesperson

Source C: Letters To The Editor

Source D: Statistical Survey

DECISION MAKING EXERCISE 2

QUESTIONS

Marks

Questions 1 to 4 are based on Sources A to D on pages 2—7. Answer Questions 1 to 4 before attempting Question 5.

In Questions 1 to 4, use only the sources described in each question.

Question 1

(*a*) Use **only** *Source A and Source C2.*

"*The new system of health care will protect patients from any such measures.*" (Lines 19–20)

What arguments might John Andrews put forward to challenge this view?   **3**

(*b*) Use **only** *Source A and Source D5.*

"*. . . Trust hospitals run their affairs like private businesses.*" (Line 24)

To what extent does the information, in Source D5, support the Government's reply, in Source A, to this claim?   **3**

Question 2

Use **only** *Source B, Source D1 and Source D2.*

Quote an example of an exaggerated sentence from Source B. Give reasons for your choice.   **3**

Question 3

Use **only** *Source C1, Source D3 and Source D4.*

What evidence is there that Marian Yule has been selective in her use of facts?   **3**

Question 4

Use **only** *Source C1 and Source C2.*

Compare the views of Marian Yule and John Andrews on the extent of democracy in the new system of health care.   **3**

(15)

Marks

Question 5

DECISION MAKING TASK

You are a civil servant from an overseas country on a fact finding visit to the Scottish Office. Your particular remit is health care. Prepare a report to send to your Government Minister of Health on the advisability of introducing an internal market into your own national system of state-funded health care.

In your report you should:

* recommend whether or not your Government should introduce an internal market into its national system of state-funded health care;

* provide arguments to support your recommendation;

* brief your Minister of Health about any criticisms your recommendation might attract **and** provide advice on answering them.

In your report you **must** use:

* the **source material** provided and

* other **background knowledge**.

Your answer should be written in a style appropriate to a *report*.

The written and statistical information sources which have been provided are as follows:

SOURCE A: Newspaper Editorial

SOURCE B: Statement by a Health Union Spokesperson

SOURCE C: Letters to the Editor

SOURCE D: Statistical Survey

(35)

Total 50 Marks

SOURCE A: NEWSPAPER EDITORIAL

A MEDICAL MARKETPLACE

The Government has always claimed the objective of its NHS reforms is to put people first. The aims are to provide better health care and improved services to patients and to give people working in the NHS greater job satisfaction. The NHS is being made more efficient in using taxpayers'
5   money. To do this the Government has introduced a limited form of market competition, with hospitals competing amongst themselves for money.

The Government calls this new system an "internal market" which will force hospitals to improve services to attract more patients and therefore stay in business. In theory, a hospital's income will depend upon how much
10   treatment it gives and the prices it charges. For instance, a hospital which performs five heart operations a week should earn five times as much as a hospital which performs only one at the same price.

Under the old funding system, a Scottish hospital was given an annual sum of money from the Government through its Health Board. If it was well-run and
15   efficient, and regularly monitored its performance, it was likely to treat a greater number of patients over the same period of time than a less efficient unit. This resulted in the more efficient hospital running out of money for operations before the financial year ended. It was then forced to start reducing its costs by cutting beds or cancelling operations. The new system of health
20   care will protect patients from any such measures.

The most heated debate over the Government's reforms has focused on this question of allowing hospitals to manage themselves. These "self-governing Trusts" are said to have "opted out" of Health Board control. The Labour Party claims that Trust hospitals run their affairs like private businesses.
25   They are no longer part of the NHS.

In reply to such accusations, the Government insists that Trusts will be non-profit making units but with the opportunity to improve patient care with greatly increased revenue from all sources. They may be outside the bureaucracy of the health service but remain very much part of the NHS.
30   Furthermore, the underlying principles of the NHS remain unchanged. Patients will still be treated free of charge. There is no possibility of a two-tier health service.

Nearly every country in the developed world is searching for the best formula on which to organise health care. They will be looking with interest to see if
35   Britain is heading in the right or wrong direction.

Source: Adapted from *Education Guardian*, 25.6.91

SOURCE B: STATEMENT BY A HEALTH UNION SPOKESPERSON

Much of the media and public attention paid to the NHS reforms has focused on NHS Trusts. While important, this aspect of the changes foreseen in Working for Patients is dwarfed in significance by the consequences of the creation of an internal market in the health service. The internal market is
5   rapidly reshaping the NHS. The nature, scope and quality of its services are being fundamentally changed; the principles upon which it was founded are being undermined. The internal market has transformed the problems experienced by the health service into a crisis. It has intensified existing financial pressures arising from underfunding.

10   Working for Patients gave many assurances about its proposals. These have all been broken. The public was assured that the changes would maintain the principles on which the NHS was founded. In reality they are steadily being eroded, with the ideals of equal access, comprehensiveness and treatment according to need and not ability to pay, gradually giving way to financial
15   considerations. Patients were told that their needs would always be considered first. Increasingly their interests are taking second place to the financial interests of Trusts and GP fundholders.

Staff have similarly been betrayed. They were told that they would receive greater satisfaction and rewards. Instead, they have been moved into a new
20   era of insecurity and low pay and often face threats to their terms and conditions of employment. The broad effect of the internal market is to construct a low paid workforce with little consideration being given to the wider social implications of such changes.

The internal market is not the solution to the difficulties of the health service.
25   Indeed it makes them worse. The internal market requires providers of services to compete against one another to win contracts. Providers must win contracts to stay afloat. If contracts are not won, unprofitable activities are closed down. The cut-throat logic of the market has been introduced. The consequences have been huge losses of acute beds by every Health Board and
30   increases in all categories of patients waiting for treatment.

We believe that for effective patient care to be provided, the internal market should be abolished. In its place should be a patient-centred NHS based on quality, equality and co-operation rather than cost-cutting, competition and conflict.

Source: Adapted from *The Market Menace,*
UNISON Health Care, January 1994.

SOURCE C: LETTERS TO THE EDITOR

C1

SIR: Speak to any Trust chief executive and they will tell you how enthusiastic they are about the freedoms Trust status gives them. Decision-making is quicker and much more local. Democracy, accountability, economy and those in need of treatment are all winners in the new system of health care. Trust and Health Board
5   members are drawn equally from a wide variety of backgrounds. All Trusts are required by law to hold public meetings within their first year.

In our own local Trust, arrangements have been made to give our GPs direct access to a new scanner for diagnosing brain disease and other disorders without their patients having to be seen by a consultant. This will cut the waiting time for such a
10   procedure. Patients are benefiting from the extension of operating sessions at the weekends. X-ray sessions are being held in the evenings, making them more convenient for people who work during the day. Some consultants are running pain clinics and asthma clinics in the evenings. This can be done because the Trust has the flexibility to pay staff for such duties. Those who would cry "market menace" are
15   blind to the advantages of a system in which money is saved and the only loser is bureaucracy.

Marian Yule

C2

SIR: Seven months ago we were shocked at the news of our local Trust hospital being told to stop doing non-emergency operations just five months into the financial year. It had fulfilled its contract too quickly.

I note with dismay that now it is to begin closing wards in a bid to find efficiency
5   savings demanded by the Health Board before it will sign new contracts. Anyone in the 120 beds affected will have to be moved whatever condition they are in. Furthermore, it appears that staff are being threatened with the loss of their jobs if they do not accept reduced employment rights. Those whose temporary contracts are nearing the two year mark have been sent letters by post offering new terms.
10   Contracts will only be renewed if they sign an agreement to give up their rights to redundancy money and protection from unfair dismissal.

May I remind you that our local Trust started in the worst possible circumstances with polls showing that the vast majority of staff and local people were opposed to change. There was no public meeting last year and Community Health Council
15   representatives have not been allowed to attend board meetings. Do competition and secrecy go hand in hand in this new system of health care ?

John Andrews

SOURCE D: STATISTICAL SURVEY

Table D1
Number of Acute Hospital Beds in Scotland 1979 and 1992 by Health Board

Health Board	1979	1992
Argyll	1279	1231
Ayrshire & Arran	918	1075
Borders	304	344
Dumfries & Galloway	418	408
Fife	682	788
Forth Valley	595	572
Grampian	1627	1410
Greater Glasgow	4314	3311
Highland	920	700
Lanarkshire	1561	1494
Lothian	2698	2135
Orkney	208	61
Shetland	62	49
Tayside	1703	1522
Western Isles	72	85

Table D2
Numbers Awaiting Treatment in Scotland 1989–1993

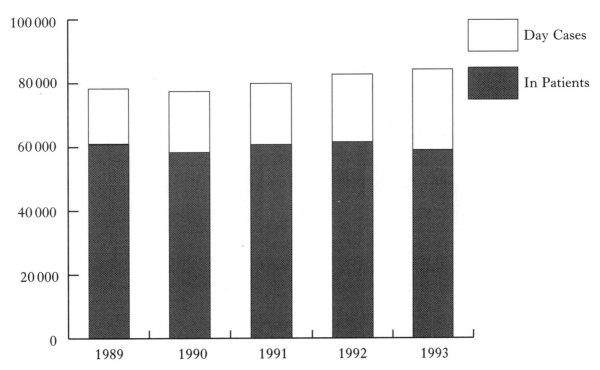

Table D3
The Rise and Fall of National Health Service Staff in Scotland 1980–1992

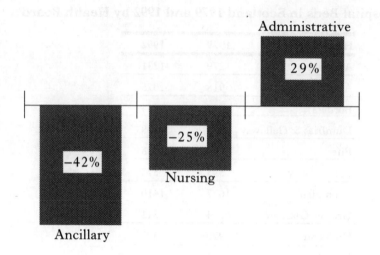

Table D4
Membership of Trust and Health Boards in Scotland 1992:
Number of People by Occupation

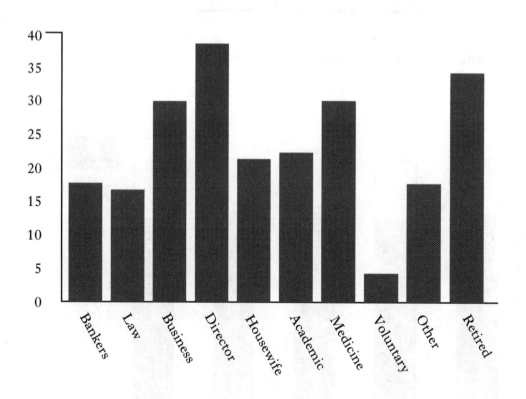

Table D5
Income and Expenditure Projections of a Scottish Trust Hospital 1995–1998

	1995–1996 £000s	1996–1997 £000s	1997–1998 £000s
Income			
Contracts with Health Board	23,338	23,122	23,206
GP Fundholders	628	851	1,088
Other Purchasers	325	280	235
Non-patient Income	1,058	1,081	1,112
Total Income	**25,349**	**25,334**	**25,641**
Expenditure			
Pay	16,821	16,733	16,757
Supplies	5,607	5,577	5,585
Depreciation	942	960	1,007
Interest	1979	2,064	2,292
Total Expenditure	**25,349**	**25,334**	**25,641**

[END OF QUESTION PAPER]

SCOTTISH
CERTIFICATE OF
EDUCATION
1996

THURSDAY, 16 MAY
9.30 AM – 12.00 NOON

MODERN STUDIES
HIGHER GRADE
Paper I

SECTION A—Politics in a Democratic Society (Study Theme 1)

Answer ONE question from this Section

Marks

Question A1

(a) Describe Conservative Party policy on **three** of the following:

employment;

public and private ownership;

health;

education;

taxation. **15**

(b) Compare the internal organisation of the Labour Party with that of the Conservative Party. **10**

(25)

Question A2

Study Reference Diagram QA2 and answer the questions which follow.

Reference Diagram QA2: UK 1992 General Election—Actual Result and Result Using Single Transferable Vote

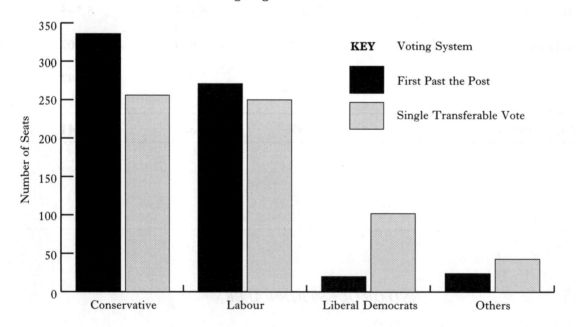

(a) Discuss the main criticisms of the "first past the post" UK electoral system. **10**

(b) Describe the possible disadvantages of changing to a system of proportional representation.

(In your answer you should refer to different systems of proportional representation.) **15**

(25)

Marks

Question A3

(a) Describe the various ways in which pressure groups, **other than the media**, may influence political decisions in the UK.

15

(b) Examine the influence of the media on voters in the UK.

10

(25)

Question A4

"Parliament is in decline; its power and authority have been transferred to the Prime Minister and Cabinet."

To what extent does Parliament influence the powers of the Prime Minister and Cabinet?

(25)

Question A5

(a) Describe the ways in which Scotland is administered within the UK system of government.

13

(b) Discuss the proposals of the political parties for reforming the way in which Scotland is governed.

12

(25)

Question A6

(a) Describe the new system of local government introduced in Scotland in 1996.

6

(b) For what reasons did the Conservative Government decide to reform the system of local government in Scotland?

9

(c) Discuss criticisms of these reforms.

10

(25)

**SECTION B—Income and Wealth in a Democratic Society (Study Theme 2),
Health Care in a Democratic Society (Study Theme 3)**

Answer ONE question from this Section

Marks

Question B7

"There is disagreement over the extent to which social class is still important in the UK. Soon after he became Prime Minister, John Major claimed we were now a classless society. However, differences in income have increased since 1979. Some claim that a new underclass has been created."

Discuss.

(25)

Question B8

(a) *"Governments have done little to improve the social and economic position of ethnic minorities and women in the UK."*

Choose **one** of the following groups:

ethnic minorities;

women.

Describe the ways in which the group which you have chosen experiences social and economic disadvantage in the UK.

15

(b) Examine recent attempts by the UK Government to improve the social and economic position of the group you have chosen.

10

(25)

Question B9

Study Reference Diagram QB9 and answer the questions which follow.

Reference Diagram QB9: Regional Differences in Unemployment in Scotland

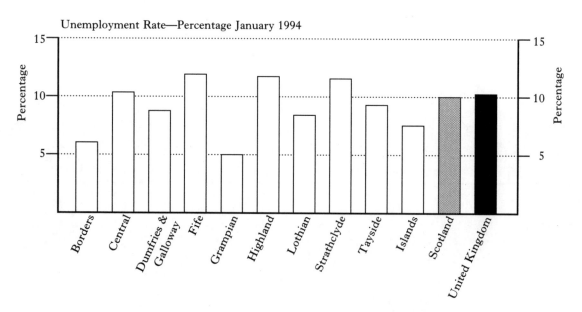

Unemployment Rate—Percentage January 1994

Source: *Regional Trends* 1994

(a) Describe the differences in unemployment between different regions in Scotland. What are the reasons for these differences?

15

(b) Examine the effects of unemployment on living standards.

10

(25)

Marks

Question B10

(*a*) What reforms has the Government introduced to improve patient choice and rights in the National Health Service in recent years? **13**

(*b*) Why have critics claimed that the National Health Service is no longer in safe hands? **12**

(25)

Question B11

(*a*) What evidence is there of health inequalities in the UK? **15**

(*b*) Examine the Government's response to inequalities in health in recent years. **10**

(25)

Question B12

(*a*) Describe the role of interested organisations and pressure groups in the provision of health care in the UK. (You may refer to Health Boards, Health Councils and the British Medical Association in your answer.) **15**

(*b*) To what extent do the health care policies of the opposition parties differ from those of the Government? **10**

Do i have enough information on policies?

(25)

Do you refer to statistics / Datas that are given in your question.

1996

SECTION C—International Issues

Answer TWO questions from this Section

Please note that within each Study Theme a choice is provided.

Answer only ONE question in relation to a single Study Theme.

REGIONAL AND NATIONAL CONFLICT (STUDY THEME 4)

Question C13   *Marks*

EITHER A   South Africa

Study Reference Data QC13A and answer the questions which follow.

Reference Data QC13A: South Africa—Selected Socio-economic Data

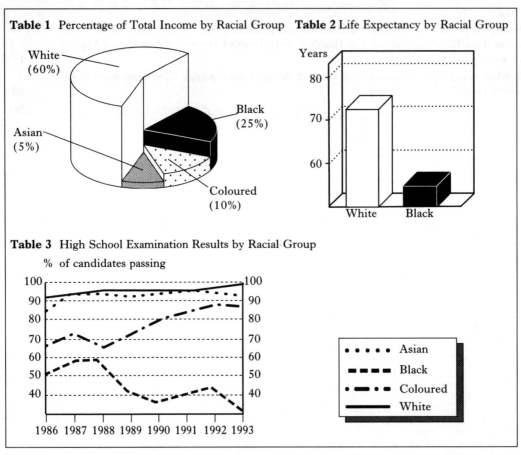

Table 1 Percentage of Total Income by Racial Group   **Table 2** Life Expectancy by Racial Group

Table 3 High School Examination Results by Racial Group

Sources: *The Economist* and *The Guardian*

A. (a) To what extent has there been social and economic progress for the non-white population of South Africa?   15

(b) Describe the political problems which have arisen in South Africa since the election of the Government of National Unity.   10

(25)

OR B   Arab-Israeli Conflict

B. (a) Describe the social and economic problems of Palestinians living in:

Israel, the West Bank, Gaza Strip and neighbouring countries.   15

(b) Examine the reactions of the various Palestinian groups to recent attempts at reaching peace with Israel.   10

(25)

MINORITIES (STUDY THEME 5)

Marks

Question C14

EITHER A   National and Religious Minorities in the Soviet Union and its Successor States

A.   (*a*)   To what extent have the former republics of the USSR been affected by ethnic conflict? (You should refer to at least **two** republics.)   **15**

(*b*)   Compare the attitudes to religion in the independent republics with attitudes which existed when they were part of the USSR.   **10**

OR B   Ethnic Minorities in the USA   **(25)**

B.   (*a*)   Describe the distribution of the Black and Hispanic populations within the USA.   **10**

(*b*)   To what extent do ethnic minorities experience social, economic and political disadvantage in the USA?   **15**

(25)

INTERNATIONAL COOPERATION AND CONFLICT (STUDY THEME 6)

Question C15

EITHER A   The European Community

Study Reference Map QC15A and answer the questions which follow.

Reference Map QC15A: Changes in Membership of the European Union

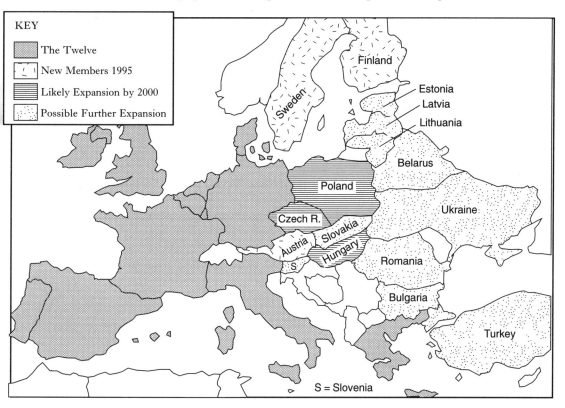

A.   (*a*)   What problems and benefits may arise for the European Union from an increase in its membership?   **13**

(*b*)   Examine the main features of the Common Agricultural Policy.   **12**

OR B   The United Nations   **(25)**

B.   (*a*)   Describe the aims and methods used by the Security Council of the United Nations. **10**

(*b*)   **With reference to specific world troublespots**, describe the criticisms made of the peacekeeping role of the UN in recent years.   **15**

(25)

IDEOLOGY AND DEVELOPMENT (STUDY THEME 7)

Marks

Question C16

EITHER A   The USA

A. (*a*) What social and economic problems have arisen from the operation of the market economy in the USA?   **13**

   (*b*) Examine social welfare policies in the USA.   **12**

                                                    (25)

OR B   Russia

B. (*a*) To what extent does Russia have a free-market economy?   **10**

   (*b*) **Other than ethnic unrest**, describe the recent social problems which have arisen in Russia.   **15**

                                                    (25)

OR C   China

C. (*a*) To what extent has the Government of China abandoned its traditional Communist principles?   **15**

   (*b*) Describe the political problems which have faced the leaders of the Chinese Communist Party in recent years.   **10**

                                                    (25)

POLITICS OF THE ENVIRONMENT (STUDY THEME 8)

Question C17

EITHER A   The Politics of Energy

A. (*a*) Describe the energy policies of political parties in the UK.   **15**

   (*b*) Examine the view that continued development and use of nuclear energy is inevitable.   **10**

                                                    (25)

OR B   The Politics of Food

B. **With reference to either North East Africa (excluding Egypt) or Southern Africa, answer the questions below.**

   (*a*) *"Rich countries give aid but take back far more in debt repayments and by paying low prices for the goods of less developed countries."*

      Discuss.   **12**

   (*b*) Describe the ways in which international agencies encourage food production and distribution.   **13**

                                                    (25)

[END OF QUESTION PAPER]

SCOTTISH
CERTIFICATE OF
EDUCATION
1996

THURSDAY, 16 MAY
1.30 PM – 4.00 PM

MODERN STUDIES
HIGHER GRADE
Paper II
Decision Making Exercise 1

Attempt:

Either   Decision Making Exercise 1:   Income and Wealth in a Democratic Society;

Or   Decision Making Exercise 2: Health Care in a Democratic Society but **not both**. The Decision making Exercises are contained in separate booklets.

A summary of the exercise is provided on the cover of each booklet.

Read the summaries carefully before deciding which exercise to attempt. In each case, answer **all** questions.

DECISION MAKING EXERCISE 1 :

INCOME AND WEALTH IN A DEMOCRATIC SOCIETY

Summary of Decision Making Exercise

You are a senior civil servant from an overseas country. Your Government is keen to reduce poverty in your country and has asked you to prepare a report in which you recommend a system based either on the policies of the UK Conservative Government or the Labour Party. (Question 5)

Before beginning the task, you must answer a number of evaluating questions (Questions 1–4) based on the source material provided. The source material is as follows:

             SOURCE A: Tackling Poverty in the UK—A Conservative Party Viewpoint

             SOURCE B: A Labour Party View of Poverty in the UK

             SOURCE C: Statistical Survey

             SOURCE D: Letter Page

DECISION MAKING EXERCISE 1

QUESTIONS

Marks

Questions 1 to 4 are based on Sources A to D on pages 2—7. Answer Questions 1 to 4 before attempting Question 5.

In Questions 1 to 4, use <u>only</u> the sources described in each question.

Question 1

(a) *Use* **only** *Source D1 and Source C1.*

To what extent can Sir James Duncan be accused of exaggeration in his comments on unemployment?

2

(b) *Use* **only** *Source A and Source B.*

Contrast the views of the Conservative Party and Labour Party on the subject of Wages Councils.

2

Question 2

Use **only** *Source C5.*

Give evidence **for** and **against** Councillor McCabe's statement in Source D2 that *the Government has changed the benefits that applied to children and replaced them with new means tested ones.*

2

Question 3

(a) *Use* **only** *Source D1 and Source C5.*

To what extent is Sir James Duncan's opinion on the Conservatives' attitude to means testing selective in its use of facts?

2

(b) *Use* **only** *Source D2 and Source B.*

To what extent is Councillor McCabe's opinion on the Labour Party's attitude to raising tax to pay for Social Security selective in its use of facts?

2

Question 4

(a) *Use* **only** *Source D1, Source D2, Source C2 and Source C3.*

Give evidence **against** the views held by Councillor McCabe **and** Sir James Duncan on poverty.

3

(b) *Use* **only** *Source D1, Source D2 and Source C4.*

Give evidence **against** the views held by Councillor McCabe **and** Sir James Duncan on personal income taken by Social Security and direct taxes.

2

(15)

Marks

Question 5

DECISION MAKING TASK

You are a senior civil servant from an overseas country. Your Government is keen to reduce poverty in your country and has asked you to prepare a report in which you recommend a system based either on the policies of the UK Conservative Government or the Labour Party.

In your report you should:

*   recommend a system based on either the Conservative Government or Labour Party policies;

*   provide arguments to support your recommendation;

*   describe any difficulties or cost implications which might follow from your recommendations.

In your report you **must** use:

*   the **source material** provided and

*   other **background knowledge**.

Your answer should be written in a style appropriate to a *report*.

The written and statistical information sources which have been provided are as follows:

SOURCE A: Tackling Poverty in the UK—A Conservative Party Viewpoint

SOURCE B: A Labour Party View of Poverty in the UK

SOURCE C: Statistical Survey

SOURCE D: Letter Page

(35)

Total: 50 Marks

SOURCE A: TACKLING POVERTY IN THE UK – A CONSERVATIVE PARTY VIEWPOINT

The Conservative Government has tackled the problem of poverty in the UK by creating greater wealth in the economy and by targeting benefits to those who really need them. As new jobs are created people are becoming even less dependent on benefits.

5   The welfare state has proved far more expensive than anyone expected. Social Security is now the biggest item of Government spending: £83,000 million in 1994–95. This is due to the increase in the number of people claiming— especially the elderly, single parents, the long term sick and the disabled.

Conservative thinking on Social Security aims to:
10   provide a reasonable income for those in genuine need;
         ensure that those who can work do so by increasing incentives to work;
         keep the cost at an affordable level and avoid waste.

A successful economy means greater wealth creation. We are achieving this by making the UK attractive to investors by scrapping practices that kept wage
15 levels artificially high, such as Wages Councils. Evidence of our success is shown in recent Department of Trade figures which indicate that wage levels in trades which had Wages Councils have now risen by more than the average in the year to 1994. Furthermore, the percentage increase in employment in these sectors has been above the rate for the rest of the country.

20 We will continue to resist the introduction of a minimum wage which would mean big increases in costs for industry and higher levels of unemployment. Similarly, John Major has successfully kept the European Union's Social Chapter out of the UK. This would have provided benefits which seem generous but which could only have been paid for by increased redundancies.

25 Much more effort now goes into catching those who try to claim benefits which they are not entitled to, as fraud costs the country millions of pounds. The unemployed are encouraged to look for work through a range of training schemes and there has been a change from Unemployment Benefit to Jobseekers Allowance. We have recently announced our intention to add to
30 the Jobseekers' Allowance by introducing local variations to benefits.

While we accept that there are sections of our society still living in poverty, figures must be set in context. Taking the poorest tenth of the population by income, 86% have a washing machine, 65% a video recorder and 53% a car. This shows that our policies are gradually dealing with the problem of poverty
35 in the UK.

SOURCE B: A LABOUR PARTY VIEW OF POVERTY IN THE UK

The Labour Party want to ensure that those in need will receive help without increasing tax for the majority of voters. With this in mind we set up the Commission on Social Justice after the 1992 General Election. Its task was to advise on how to modernise the welfare state. The first finding of the
5   Commission was that poverty had risen in the UK in the 1980s. Overall one fifth of the UK population now lives in poverty.

We believe that the key to eliminating poverty does not lie only in providing benefits but by raising pay levels. The cost of low pay falls not only on the employee but also on the taxpayer. There have been increases in the number
10   of women workers and part-time jobs, both of which are associated with low pay. The cost of providing benefits, such as Family Credit, Income Support and Housing Benefit, for those in work has doubled over the past four years and now stands at £2·4 billion per year. Topping-up benefits for the low paid should not be an incentive for the employer to cut pay and leave the taxpayer
15   to pay the bill. This is a clear argument for a minimum wage.

The Conservatives' main attack on the minimum wage is that it will cost jobs and deter inward investment. There is no evidence to support either of these claims. Evidence from many countries which have minimum wage laws, such as the USA, suggests they have stronger rates of employment growth than
20   Britain. One survey of companies coming to Britain showed they were attracted by the quality of our workforce and our facilities.

It is also important to re-establish Wage Councils. Over 78% of jobs advertised in catering, shops, clothes industry and hairdressing are paying less than the income support poverty line, with almost all part-time jobs and
25   nearly half the full-time posts falling below that level.

Conservative policies have made it more difficult for people to get Social Security benefits and have attempted to reduce fraud. The amount not claimed by those who are entitled to do so is greater than that lost through fraud, which shows some of the problems of means testing. We would mount
30   a campaign to encourage the needy to claim. Large sums of money are also lost through tax avoidance. This we would also seek to change.

The suggested changes to the Jobseekers' Allowance signal the Conservative Party's desire to break up the benefits system. It is essential to introduce the Social Chapter, with its generous social benefits, which is enjoyed by other
35   countries in the European Union. Many of these countries have stronger economies than the UK.

At present low wages mean that too many UK workers are in the "poverty trap"—discouraged from looking for a job as they are little better off working than being on benefits. Higher wages would make this less common. Benefits
40   should be used more to "top-up" low or part-time wages. However, benefits should be taxable as that would take money back from the better off without forcing the poor to go through a means test.

SOURCE C: STATISTICAL SURVEY

Source C1:   Unemployment in the United Kingdom

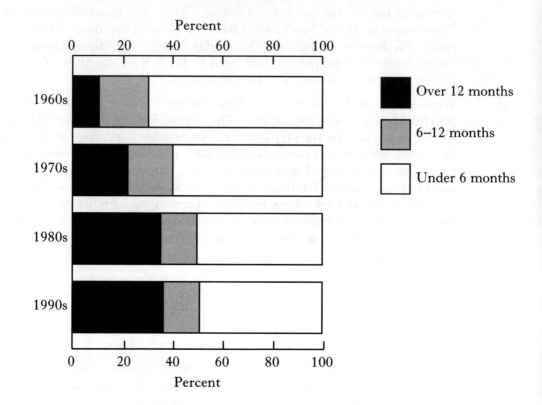

Source C2:   Poverty in the UK 1979–92

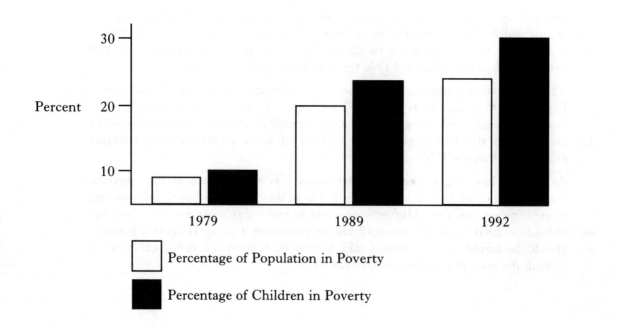

Source C3: **Percentage of Households in Poverty—Selected Countries 1988**

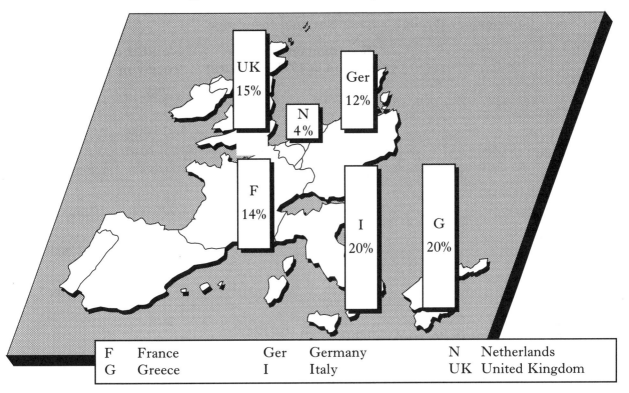

F	France	Ger	Germany	N	Netherlands
G	Greece	I	Italy	UK	United Kingdom

Source C4: **Percentage of Personal Income Taken by Social Security Contribution and Direct Taxes—Selected Countries 1991**

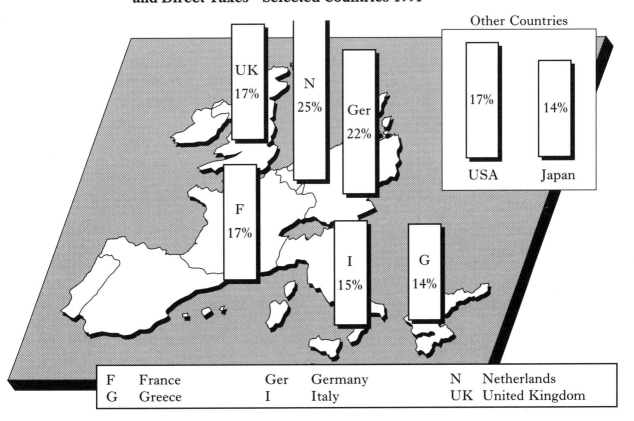

F	France	Ger	Germany	N	Netherlands
G	Greece	I	Italy	UK	United Kingdom

Source C5:   Major Social Security Benefits—1982–93

C5 (a)   Contributory through paying National Insurance

	Spending on Benefits (£ million at 1992–93 prices)		Number of persons receiving benefits	
	1982	**1993**	**1982**	**1993**
Retirement Pension	22,356	26,856	9,015,000	9,910,000
Invalidity Benefit	2,526	6,100	660,000	1,490,000
Unemployment Benefit	3,138	1,838	1,220,000	715,000
Sickness Benefit	1,254	315	445,000	135,000
Statutory Sick Pay **	—	710	—	330,000

C5 (b)   Non-Contributory—Available to all

	Spending on Benefits (£ million at 1992–93 prices)		Number of persons receiving benefits	
	1982	**1993**	**1982**	**1993**
Child Benefit	6,217	5,767	13,145,000	12,485,000

C5 (c)   Income Related—Means Tested

	Spending on Benefits (£ million at 1992–93 prices)		Number of persons receiving benefits	
	1982	**1993**	**1982**	**1993**
Supplementary Pension/Allowance *	8,923	—	3,725,000	—
Income Support **	—	14,461	—	5,320,000
Family Income Supplement *	122	—	125,000	—
Family Credit **	—	864	—	420,000
Housing Benefit & Rebates	1,036	3,520	1,840,000	4,315,000

** Benefit introduced after 1982   * Benefit discontinued after 1982

Source: Social Trends 1994

SOURCE D: LETTER PAGE

Source D1

SIR:

As a businessman who often travels abroad, I wish to point out some of the problems caused by the cost of Social Security. It is the biggest burden on taxpayers and it is getting worse. In the past most benefits were handed out without any attempt to check if they were needed. This was clearly misguided. After all, apart from the old folk, there are very few genuinely poor people in the country today. Indeed, the percentage of families in poverty is lower in the UK than the rest of the European Union. I accept unemployment is high but the Conservatives have introduced training schemes which mean fewer people are out of work for a long time.

To fight poverty we are paying a bigger contribution from our personal income to the state than any of our competitors. This discourages both business and workers who are, after all, the people we need to build up our economy.

Thank goodness the Conservatives are now sorting out the scroungers by making all these benefits means tested, apart from the old age pension!

Sir James Duncan

Source D2

SIR:

The failure of the Conservatives to introduce a minimum wage is a scandal. Worse still, they have cut back spending on benefits during a recession. Most benefits are now means tested and many people do not claim. This, of course, is the main reason why so many old people are poor. As for families, the Government has changed the benefits that applied to children and replaced them with new means tested ones. As a result we have record levels of poverty which are the worst in the European Union.

It is no use the Tories claiming we can't pay better benefits because we need to compete with other countries. Every other country in the European Union is more generous to its poorer citizens. Citizens in the most successful world economies, like Germany and Japan, happily pay a much greater proportion of their personal earnings in tax, to help provide decent Social Security, than we do in the UK.

Thankfully, the Labour Party is still committed to providing adequate Social Security whatever the cost in taxation!

Councillor Rachel McCabe

[END OF QUESTION PAPER]

SCOTTISH
CERTIFICATE OF
EDUCATION
1996

THURSDAY, 16 MAY
1.30 PM – 4.00 PM

MODERN STUDIES
HIGHER GRADE
Paper II
Decision Making Exercise 2

Attempt:

Either   Decision Making Exercise 1: Income and Wealth in a Democratic Society;

Or   Decision Making Exercise 2: Health Care in a Democratic Society but **not both**. The Decision making Exercises are contained in separate booklets.

A summary of the exercise is provided on the cover of each booklet.

Read the summaries carefully before deciding which exercise to attempt. In each case, answer **all** questions.

DECISION MAKING EXERCISE 2:

HEALTH CARE IN A DEMOCRATIC SOCIETY

Summary of Decision Making Exercise

You are a Health Policy Researcher. Prepare a report for submission to Annfield Health Council on the desirability of General Practitioners at Annfield Grove becoming part of the General Practice Fundholding Scheme (Question 5).

Before beginning the task, you must answer a number of evaluating questions (Questions 1–4) based on the source material provided. The source material is as follows:

       Source A: Government Press Release

       Source B: Opposition Press Release

       Source C: Letter Page

       Source D: Statistical Survey

DECISION MAKING EXERCISE 2

QUESTIONS

Marks

Questions 1 to 4 are based on Sources A to D on pages 2—7. Answer Questions 1 to 4 before attempting Question 5.

In Questions 1 to 4, use only the sources described in each question.

Question 1

*Use **only** Source A, Source D1 and Source D2.*

Quote an example of exaggeration from Source A. Give reasons for your choice.   **3**

Question 2

*Use **only** Source A and Source D6.*

To what extent does the evidence support the Government's reply to claims about the real cost of the biggest savings to be made on hospital procedures?   **4**

Question 3

(*a*) *Use **only** Source C1 and Source B.*

Find two pieces of evidence in support of J Raeburn's claim about the Department of Health guidelines.   **2**

(*b*) *Use **only** Source C1 and Source C2.*

Compare the views of J Raeburn and R Morris on why hospital waiting lists are so long in certain areas.   **2**

(*c*) *Use **only** Source C2 and Source D3.*

Why might R Morris be accused of being selective in his use of facts to justify his claim about the popularity of the Fundholding scheme?   **2**

Question 4

*Use **only** Source D4 and Source D5.*

"*. . . for some equipment, Fundholders are more generously financed than non-Fundholders, but the ways in which practice savings can be made remain a mystery.*"

To what extent does the evidence support the points being made in this statement?   **2**

(15)

Question 5

DECISION MAKING TASK

You are a Health Policy Researcher. Prepare a report for submission to Annfield Health Council on the desirability of General Practitioners at Annfield Grove becoming part of the General Practice Fundholding Scheme.

In your report you should:

* recommend either participation or non-participation in the scheme;
* provide arguments to support your recommendation;
* identify and comment on any economic, social and political arguments which may be presented by those who oppose your recommendation.

In your report you **must** use:

* the **source material** provided and
* other **background knowledge**.

Your answer should be written in a style appropriate to a *report*.

The written and statistical information sources which have been provided are as follows:

SOURCE A: Government Press Release

SOURCE B: Opposition Press Release

SOURCE C: Letter Page

SOURCE D: Statistical Survey

(35)

Total 50 Marks

SOURCE A: GOVERNMENT PRESS RELEASE

The White Paper "Working For Patients" recognised that GPs were "uniquely placed to improve patients' choice of good quality services" because of their relationship with patients and hospitals. The principal aim of the General Practice Fundholding Scheme is to build on this unique situation so
5   that patients can benefit. The latest figures show that the number of Fundholders in Scotland has increased at the same spectacular annual rate since 1992, thus bringing the potential for improved patient care to the majority of patients nationwide.

Changes announced today underline the Government's growing commitment
10   to Fundholding in Scotland and to seeing its benefits spread quickly. While Fundholding will remain a voluntary scheme, all practices will be given the opportunity to join and secure the direct benefits of primary care-led purchasing for their patients. The GP patient list size for entry into standard Fundholding will reduce from 6,000 to 4,000 patients in Scotland. This will
15   allow just over half of GP practices in Scotland to participate within the scheme without having to group with larger practices. Fundholding is a key element in developing a patient sensitive NHS. It gives more power and responsibility to family doctors. It enables them to decide in their own surgeries how best to improve services for patients.

20   Those practices which join the Fundholding Scheme will retain the right to prescribe the types of drugs they use. Beyond that, however, there will be more opportunities for decisions about purchasing and providing health care to be taken as close to the patients as possible. Fundholders may choose the hospital to which they send their patients and pay those hospitals directly for
25   the provision of certain services. Fundholders will now be able to negotiate nearly all non-emergency, in-patient and day-care surgery, as well as almost all out-patient attendance at hospital.

Freedom to choose will enable Fundholders to expand the quality and range of services they provide, drive down waiting times and make savings. Once the
30   Fundholding GP has met all their patients' needs, any savings made may be used to benefit the practice. The public may remain confident that this freedom is backed by proper accountability. To ensure that Fundholders use taxpayers' money responsibly, there are rules on the use of savings for the benefit of patients. Claims that the biggest savings to be made on hospital
35   procedures will be at the real cost of inconvenience to either the patient or their family, are completely without foundation.

SOURCE B: OPPOSITION PRESS RELEASE

Most of the attention on the Government's GP Fundholding scheme has focused on the creation of a two-tier system. This has meant better access to hospital care for patients of Fundholding GPs, compared to those from non-Fundholding GPs. Many hospitals are now taking patients from
5   Fundholding practices ahead of other patients with similar needs for urgent treatment. Some Fundholders even have hospital consultants visiting the practice. Patients in such practices are effectively jumping the queue by avoiding the long wait endured by out-patients from non-Fundholding practices.

10   Consultants complain of being torn between the financial pressure to "fast-track" patients of Fundholders and the moral pressure not to do so. Even hospital managers have apologised for "fast tracking". They claim it is necessary to win business from Fundholders and to keep their hospitals financially secure. The two-tier system is, clearly, widespread.

15   *   A letter has gone from the Royal Surrey County Hospital to all consultants. They are asked to provide emergency treatment for everyone but, in the area of non-acute surgery, to give priority to patients of Fundholders.

     *   Mid Downs, West Sussex, announced in January that patients on the
20   waiting list from non-Fundholding practices would not be considered for treatment until after 1st April.

     *   Basildon and Thurrock Hospitals in Essex have said that they have no more money to operate on patients from non-Fundholding practices.

     *   A Tunbridge Wells doctor was informed, by a consultant surgeon, that no
25   appointment could be found for a patient. However, had a mistake been made and the doctor was indeed a Fundholding GP, his patient could be sent an appointment.

Further concern has been expressed that, for hospital care, Fundholding practices are financed more generously than non-Fundholding practices.
30   Questioned by the Commons Select Committee on Health, the Health Secretary denied that Fundholders were more generously financed but produced no evidence to support this view. The indication was that the Government would not fund research either to confirm or deny this answer.

A programme of research is urgently needed to investigate the scheme's
35   impact to date: to identify and promote success where it genuinely exists; to remove inequalities and inefficiency wherever they may be. Without this, to expand Fundholding will be costly and reckless.

SOURCE C: LETTER PAGE

C1

SIR: Evidence suggests that the unfair and disorderly health market the Conservatives have created is allowing public resources to be squandered. The special relationship between patient, family doctor and hospitals is being destroyed. Consultants are ignoring Department of Health Guidelines which say that the timing
5 of individual patient consultation and treatment, when necessary, must be based only on clinical need. Fundholding practices have little interest in special needs groups. They are answerable to no-one as to how they conduct their financial affairs and use any savings. It is obvious that for some equipment, Fundholders are more generously financed than non-Fundholders, but the ways in which practice savings can be made
10 remain a mystery. However, it can surely be no coincidence that some of the biggest savings made by GP Fundholders have been in areas with the longest hospital waiting lists. GP Fundholding has introduced a two-tier, profit-driven service into the NHS. It should be scrapped and replaced with a properly planned approach to the provision of primary health care services.

J Raeburn

C2

SIR: I must condemn the recent suggestions that GP Fundholders are misusing public funds. Fundholding budgets are similar to those held by health authorities on behalf of non-Fundholders. The Fundholding rules are quite clear. Fundholders' accounts are examined monthly by the health authorities and are checked annually by
5 the Audit Commission before any identified savings may be used. There is no obligation to hand back surplus funds. However, most surpluses have been returned to health authorities for the general benefit of all patients. Fundholders would dearly like to use the efficiency savings to buy hospital treatment for more of their patients but this is impossible in areas where hospitals are already working at full capacity.
10 Fundholding continues to remain popular with the majority of GPs. If Fundholders are to be in the driving seat of health care, they must have petrol in the tank, which means having the resources to finance care. Does J Raeburn wish to defend the old structure of the National Health Service or improve services to patients?

R Morris

SOURCE D: STATISTICAL SURVEY

Source D1:   GP Fundholders—Number of Practices in Scotland

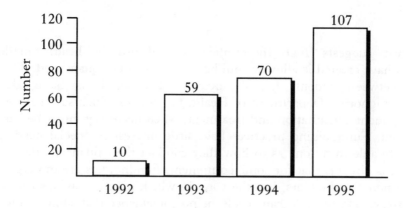

Source D2:   Percentage of Population Covered by Fundholders 1993–95

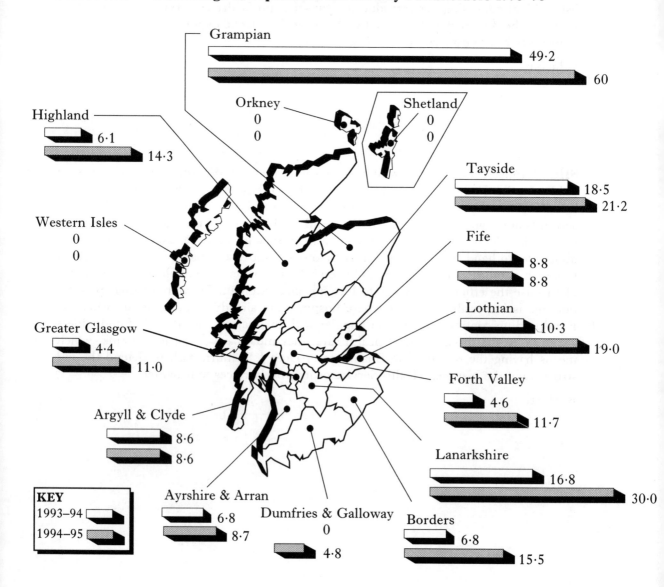

Source D3: **Support for Fundholding—Three Ballots of GPs in England and Wales 1992**

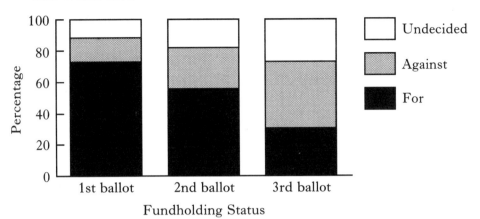

Source D4: **Financial Support for Computer Purchase in England and Wales 1991–92**

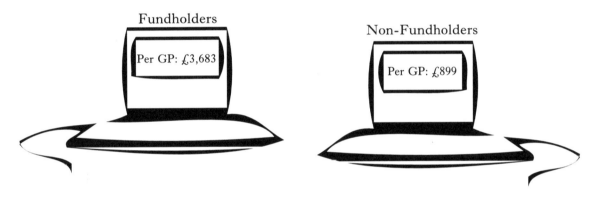

Source D5: **Savings Made by Using Generic Drugs**

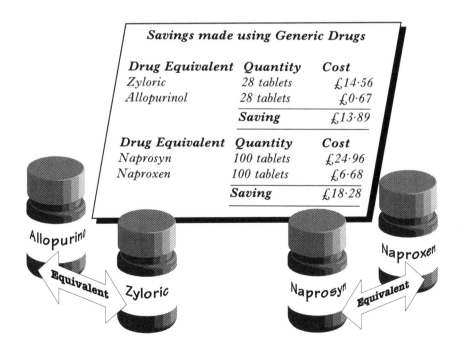

Source D6:   **Cost of Selected Health Care Procedures**

PROCEDURE	HOSPITALS & DISTANCES FROM ANNFIELD*		
	St Patrick's 128 km (80 miles)	Duncan Royal 80 km (50 miles)	St John's 32 km (20 miles)
OUT-PATIENT Seen by consultant to decide on course of treatment	£54	£351	£43
WAITING TIME	4 weeks	6 weeks	2 weeks
IN-PATIENT Removal of gall bladder by microsurgery	£1129	£1743	£1405
WAITING TIME	5 weeks	3 weeks	7 weeks

* Percentage of Households in Annfield having one car ⎹45⎸

[END OF QUESTION PAPER]

MODERN STUDIES
HIGHER GRADE
Paper I

SECTION A—Politics in a Democratic Society (Study Theme 1)

Answer ONE question from this Section

Marks

Question A1

Under the leadership of Tony Blair, many features of party policy have been reviewed to create the "new" Labour Party.

(a) Describe the changes made to Labour Party policy under the leadership of Tony Blair. **15**

(b) Discuss the ways in which Conservative Party policy is made. **10**

(25)

Question A2

Study Reference Table QA2 and answer the questions which follow.

Reference Table QA2 : % Vote by Social Class

	1987	1992	1987	1992	1987	1992	1987	1992	1987	1992
Conservative	56	55	48	50	43	41	32	31	26	27
Labour	13	23	25	29	36	40	47	55	54	56
Liberal	31	22	27	21	21	19	21	14	20	17
	Professional/ Managerial (ABs)		Office/ Clerical (C1s)		Skilled-Manual (C2s)		Semi-Skilled/ Unskilled Manual (DEs)		Unemployed	

(a) Examine the link between social class and voting behaviour in the United Kingdom. **12**

(b) Describe the other factors which may influence voting behaviour in the United Kingdom. **13**

(25)

Question A3

Pressure groups are an important way of providing the public with acceptable opportunities to influence Government decisions. However, the role of some MPs in pressure group activity has been severely criticised in recent years.

Discuss. **(25)**

Marks

Question A4

(a) Describe the part played by **both** Government and Opposition backbench MPs in controlling the Prime Minister and Cabinet. **15**

(b) Examine the role of Senior Civil Servants in the United Kingdom system of government. **10**

(25)

Question A5

(a) Describe the part played by **each** of the following in the administration of Scottish government.

(i) The Scottish Office

(ii) The Secretary of State for Scotland **13**

(b) Examine the arguments **against** an increase in devolved power for Scotland. **12**

(25)

Question A6

(a) Discuss the role of local government in a democratic society. **10**

(b) Describe the ways in which **both** the organisation and financing of local government in Scotland have changed in recent years. **15**

(25)

SECTION B—Income and Wealth in a Democratic Society (Study Theme 2), Health Care in a Democratic Society (Study Theme 3)

Answer ONE question from this Section

Marks

Question B7

(a) What evidence is there that income inequality between particular groups in British society is widening? **10**

(b) Examine the causes of income inequality in British society. **15**

(25)

Question B8

(a) *There are well-off individuals and families who do not need state benefits. The State Retirement Pension and Child Benefit should be means-tested so that additional funds are made available for the truly needy.*

Discuss. **12**

(b) In what ways do Labour and Conservative Party policies differ on the provision of help for people on low incomes? **13**

(25)

Question B9

(a) Describe the problems associated with the quality of housing in the UK. **13**

(b) Examine those factors, **other than housing**, which can affect standards of living in the UK. **12**

(25)

Question B10

(a) *There are still problems with the National Health Service. With ever expanding demands, including those of an ageing population, and with limited resources, it has become a victim of its own success.*

To what extent can the National Health Service be described as *"a victim of its own success"*? **12**

(b) What changes have been made to the responsibility for the provision of care for the elderly in the UK in recent years? **13**

(25)

internal market ?

Question B11

(a) In what ways have recent governments encouraged competition in the provision of medical care? **13**

(b) Examine the arguments **against** private health care in the UK. **12**

(25)

Question B12

(a) Discuss the causes of inequalities in health in the UK. **15**

(b) Examine the role of positive health care campaigns in improving the health of the nation. **10**

(25)

SECTION C—International Issues

Answer TWO questions from this Section

Please note that within each Study Theme a choice is provided.

Answer only ONE question in relation to a single Study Theme.

REGIONAL AND NATIONAL CONFLICT (STUDY THEME 4)

Marks

Question C13

    EITHER A   South Africa

A.   *A new South Africa is being built. A remarkably good start has been made in the face of huge social and economic problems. However, disputes between the original members of the Government of National Unity are seen as a threat to a prosperous multi-racial democracy.*

    (*a*) Describe the social and economic problems with which the South African Government has been faced **since** majority rule.   **13**

    (*b*) To what extent have there been "*disputes between the original members of the Government of National Unity*"?   **12**

                           (25)

    OR B   Arab-Israeli Conflict

B.   (*a*) Examine the role of **both** Israeli and Palestinian groups opposed to the peace process.   **12**

    (*b*) Describe the progress made towards Palestinian independence.   **13**

                           (25)

MINORITIES (STUDY THEME 5)

Question C14

EITHER A   National and Religious Minorities in the Soviet Union and its Successor States

Study Reference Map QC14A and answer the questions which follow.

Reference Map QC14A: Russia's "Near Abroad"

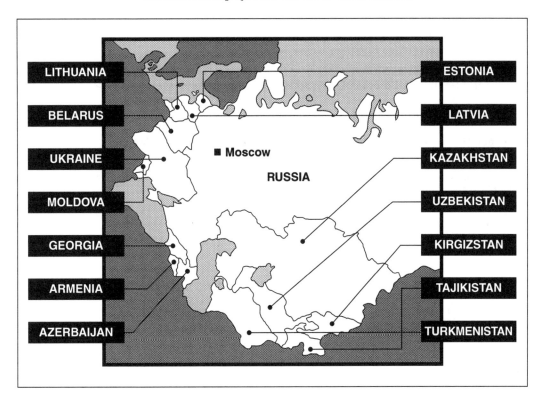

A.   (*a*) Describe Russian policy towards the republics of the "near abroad".   **13**

  (*b*) Examine the response of the Russian Government to Chechen nationalism.   **12**

       (25)

OR B   Ethnic Minorities in the USA

B.   (*a*) Affirmative Action has been the key to economic and social progress for some. However, both white and African Americans have their own reasons for being hostile to this policy.

  Discuss.   **15**

  (*b*) Describe the political progress made by ethnic minorities in recent years.   **10**

       (25)

INTERNATIONAL COOPERATION AND CONFLICT (STUDY THEME 6)

Marks

Question C15

EITHER A   The European Union

A.   (*a*) Describe the role of **each** of the following in the European Union:

the European Parliament;

the European Commission;

the Council of Ministers.   **15**

Answer either part (*b*) or part (*c*).

(*b*) Examine the success of the European Union Social Policy.   **10**

or

(*c*) To what extent has the European Union achieved a single market?   **10**

(25)

OR B   The United Nations

B.   (*a*) Examine the response of the United Nations to the crises in **two** of the following:

Rwanda;   Somalia;   Bosnia.   **15**

(*b*) What proposals have been made in recent years to improve the peace-keeping role of
the United Nations?   **10**

(25)

IDEOLOGY AND DEVELOPMENT (STUDY THEME 7)

Question C16

EITHER A   The USA

A.   (*a*) Describe the measures taken, in recent years, to deregulate the economy.   **12**

(*b*) To what extent has there been reform of the welfare system?   **13**

(25)

OR B   Russia

B.   (*a*) To what extent has there been an increase in democracy in Russia in recent years?   **10**

(*b*) Describe the social and economic factors which have brought increased popularity to
the Communist Party.   **15**

(25)

OR C   China

C.   (*a*) *The Communist leadership may have relaxed some of its economic control over the Chinese
people in recent years, but its political grip remains as tight as ever.*

Discuss.   **15**

(*b*) Describe those social problems which have accompanied China's progress towards a
market economy.   **10**

(25)

POLITICS OF THE ENVIRONMENT (STUDY THEME 8)

Marks

Question C17

    EITHER A   The Politics of Energy

A.   *(a)* Outline the arguments **both** for and against the continued use of nuclear energy.   **15**

    (b) To what extent has "green" pressure group activity influenced UK energy policy?   **10**

                          (25)

    OR B   The Politics of Food

B.   **With reference to either North East Africa (excluding Egypt) or Southern Africa, answer the questions below.**

    (a) Describe the main causes of food shortages.   **13**

    (b) Examine the role of Non-Governmental Organisations (NGOs) in preventing food shortages.   **12**

                          (25)

[END OF QUESTION PAPER]

SCOTTISH
CERTIFICATE OF
EDUCATION
1997

FRIDAY, 16 MAY
1.00 PM – 3.30 PM

MODERN STUDIES
HIGHER GRADE
Paper II
Decision Making Exercise 1

Attempt:

Either   Decision Making Exercise 1: Income and Wealth in a Democratic Society;

Or   Decision Making Exercise 2: Health Care in a Democratic Society but **not both**. The Decision Making Exercises are contained in separate booklets.

A summary of the exercise is provided on the cover of each booklet.

Read the summaries carefully before deciding which exercise to attempt. In each case, answer **all** questions.

DECISION MAKING EXERCISE 1 :

INCOME AND WEALTH IN A DEMOCRATIC SOCIETY

Summary of Decision Making Exercise

You are the Chairperson of Strathglen Council's Anti-Poverty Committee. You have been asked by the Council to decide whether or not Strathglen should volunteer to try out the new GAIN programme proposed by the Government.

Before beginning the task, you must answer a number of evaluating questions (Questions 1–5) based on the source material provided. The source material is as follows:

> **SOURCE A**:   Statement by Government Spokesperson
>
> **SOURCE B**:   Newspaper Article—Extract from Strathglen Press
>
> **SOURCE C**:   Viewpoints
>
> **SOURCE D**:   Statistical Survey

DECISION MAKING EXERCISE 1

QUESTIONS

Marks

Questions 1 to 5 are based on Sources A to D on pages 2–6. Answer Questions 1 to 5 before attempting Question 6.

In Questions 1 to 5, use <u>only</u> the sources described in each question.

Question 1

Use **only** *Source A and Source B.*

Compare the views of the Government Spokesperson and the newspaper article on lone parents living on income support.

1

Question 2

(*a*) *Use* **only** *Source D3 and Source A.*

Give evidence to support the Government Spokesperson's claims on Income Support.

2

(*b*) *Use* **only** *Source B, Source D4(a) and Source D4(b).*

What claim does the newspaper article make about the opportunities for employment? Give evidence to support this claim.

3

Question 3

Use **only** *Source C2 and Source A.*

Quote an example of exaggeration from Karen Johnstone. Give a reason for your choice.

2

Question 4

Use **only** *Source D2 and Source B.*

To what extent do the data support the viewpoints of the newspaper article?

3

Question 5

(*a*) *Use* **only** *Source C1 and Source C2.*

Compare the views of William McNally and Karen Johnstone on the standard of living of people on income support.

2

(*b*) *Use* **only** *Source D1 and Source C1.*

What evidence is there that William McNally is being selective in his use of the facts?

2

(15)

Question 6

DECISION MAKING TASK

You are the Chairperson of Strathglen Council's Anti-Poverty Committee. You have been asked by the Council to decide whether or not Strathglen should volunteer to try out the new GAIN programme proposed by the Government.

In your report you should:

* recommend either participation or non-participation in GAIN;

* provide arguments to support your recommendation;

* identify and comment on any economic, social and political arguments which may be presented by those who oppose your recommendation.

In your report you **must** use:

* the **source material** provided and

* other **background knowledge**.

Your answer should be written in a style appropriate to a *report*.

The written and statistical information sources which have been provided are as follows:

SOURCE A: Statement by Government Spokesperson
SOURCE B: Newspaper Article—Extract from Strathglen Press
SOURCE C: Viewpoints
SOURCE D: Statistical Survey

(35)

Total: 50 Marks

SOURCE A: STATEMENT BY GOVERNMENT SPOKESPERSON

We have a duty to provide the best possible future for our young people. The facts speak for themselves. Over 1 in every 6 young people are looking for employment. If we do not act, many of today's young unemployed risk becoming unemployable and we will face decades of social division. The
5   Government accepts that it has a responsibility to those people who find themselves out of work and wish to regain employment. That is why we are proposing the Greater Avenues For Independence Initiative (GAIN).

For a significant minority, previous welfare policies have created a "culture of dependency". The welfare state, and in particular Income Support, has been
10   open to abuse by those who will not take responsibility for their lives. As the numbers of people living on state assistance spiral upwards, the Government, by economic necessity, must face up to some hard choices. In particular, the present system encourages lone parenthood by providing young women with incentives to have babies and not to take jobs which are available to them. We
15   are no longer prepared to sit back and see women refuse the opportunity of part-time employment with decent pay in order to claim state benefits. Next to the registered unemployed, single mothers are the largest group claiming Income Support. We are seeking to make it easier for more and more people to raise themselves from a life of dependency. Instead of a hand out we offer a
20   hand up.

GAIN is a national initiative but it will be funded and administered by local authorities. Those authorities who volunteer to test GAIN will receive extra funding for the first three years.

Those who remain out of work after six months and who do not apply
25   **for a GAIN training course will lose 40% of their benefit**.

GAIN offers, instead of dependency, real training and a real stake in society. GAIN will:

• place trainees in a company or local authority of their choice (subject to availability) within six months;

30   • maintain living standards. Traineeships will be paid at present levels of Income Support. Free nursery places will be made available to those who have children below school age;

• offer on-the-job training and one day per week attendance at a college of Further Education. GAIN traineeships will last either one or two years
35   and win the respect of employers;

• ensure that all employers offer quality training and work experience;

• create a national "Jobs Highway". All participants will have access to the best career advice to construct their own career development plan.

Everyone unemployed for six months is guaranteed a place. With GAIN,
40   continuing forever on benefit cannot and will not be an option. The taxpayers of this country expect us to spend their hard-earned money carefully and certainly not on undeserved benefits. We also have a responsibility to promote real opportunities to work and train. The unemployed, for their part, have a responsibility to seek work. GAIN is a high quality scheme which will deliver
45   a modern welfare policy for the next century.

SOURCE B: NEWSPAPER ARTICLE—EXTRACT FROM STRATHGLEN PRESS

This Government seems determined to attack single parents and to find someone else to blame for its own mistakes. In fact, far from scrounging from the state, the Department of Social Security's own survey in 1994 showed that 91% of lone parents would work immediately or later on if they could.

5   This GAIN initiative is politically designed to appeal to the prejudices of the affluent middle class. It also tries to frighten the unemployed into low paid sweat-shops where they will be used as cheap labour for employers. We have seen from the experience of the Youth Training Scheme and the Community Programme that at the end of the training period the jobs are simply not
10   available for many young people. The unemployed just move from one training scheme to the next. Instead of helping the unemployed, GAIN will punish them. It promises a guaranteed place to all. While there may be plenty of choice of places in large cities, the unemployed in the most depressed parts of the country may have hardly any choice, if at all. Likewise, the plan to force
15   the unemployed to accept places is flawed. No company will be keen to take on trainees who do not want to be there.

The Government, instead, should do something about the "poverty trap". More publicly funded childcare places must be made available. It is the lack of decent, affordable childcare facilities in the UK that keeps young women
20   from coming off social security and getting a job. The UK has one of the poorest records on childcare in Europe. Most single mothers do not want to be dependents, but they need help from the Government to stand on their own feet.

This must be accompanied by a reform of the tax system which allows the low
25   paid to keep more of what they earn and so provide an incentive to work. Why not raise the threshold at which low earners start paying Income Tax? We should not be afraid to raise taxes a little bit in order to finance proper levels of childcare, enabling low paid women to be financially independent. The present system makes people worse off if they go out to work as it is usually
30   low paid, part-time jobs women are likely to find. Give *them*, not the comfortable middle classes, a tax break. Our European partners seem to have no problem in providing a humane system of social security. We seem obsessed with harassing the unemployed and becoming the sweat-shop of Europe!

35   In addition, we must invest in real jobs that will be of lasting good to the country. A community-led house building programme will create thousands of jobs for the unemployed. The rich, those on incomes of £60,000 or more, who have "gained" the most in the last ten years, should be more heavily taxed to finance this. The real scroungers are not single mothers but those
40   employers who increase their wealth by cutting jobs and pay in the expectation that the welfare state will pick up the tab. GAIN does not meet the real needs of the unemployed.

SOURCE C: VIEWPOINTS

Source C1: Viewpoint of William McNally

The Government is to be applauded on this initiative. Day to day life in
lower-class Britain will soon be characterised by high levels of criminality,
child neglect and drug use. Britain, like other Western democracies, has a
soaring rate of illegitimate births and can no longer afford to keep giving such
5 generous benefits to the work-shy. Single parents who live on *income
support live off the taxpayer and drain the system of every penny they can
get—legal or otherwise. The present system encourages the likes of single
mothers with boyfriends to remain unmarried and pretend to the benefit office
that they are women living alone. It infuriates me when I see people on
10 *income support having a good standard of living while we work hard for a
living and pay taxes so they can remain idle!

* "Income Support" changed to "Jobseekers' Allowance" in September 1996.

Source C2: Viewpoint of Karen Johnstone, single parent, lives in Strathglen

GAIN completely fails to understand what it's like to be poor and try to bring
up a family today. I'm 26 years old and I left my partner after he was violent
towards me. I receive £78 per week from the DSS to look after my two young
children, Stephen (6) and Debbie (3). I face a daily struggle to provide food,
5 heating and clothes for my children. One day the house was so cold that the
windows were iced up on the inside in the morning! I always buy cheap food
and sometimes miss a meal to make ends meet. With the children to look after
I see little prospect of finding work in the near future. There is nothing in
GAIN for people in my situation. If I accept a place I will lose benefits and
10 my standard of living will fall. It gets me down being a single mother.

SOURCE D: STATISTICAL SURVEY

Source D1:   Actual take-up by those entitled to claim Income Support* in Strathglen.

	1996
Overall	75%
Pensioners	67%
Non-Pensioners	81%
—couples with dependent children	85%
—one parents	94%
—others	74%

* Changed to Jobseekers' Allowance in September 1996

Source D2:   Publicly funded childcare services in the European Union for children aged 3–6 years.

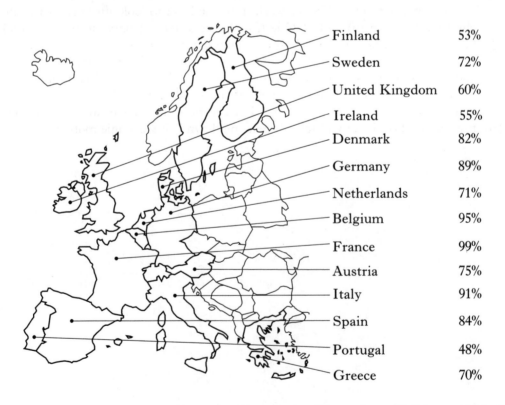

Finland	53%
Sweden	72%
United Kingdom	60%
Ireland	55%
Denmark	82%
Germany	89%
Netherlands	71%
Belgium	95%
France	99%
Austria	75%
Italy	91%
Spain	84%
Portugal	48%
Greece	70%

Source: European Commission Network on Childcare, 1990–1995

Source D3: **Categories of people who claim Income Support* in Strathglen, 1996.**

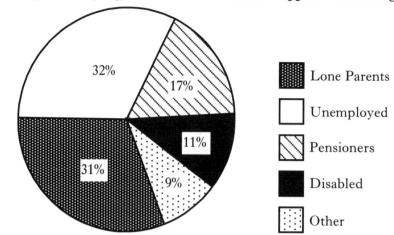

* Changed to Jobseekers' Allowance in September 1996

Source D4(a): **Destination of YT leavers in Strathglen (January 1996)**

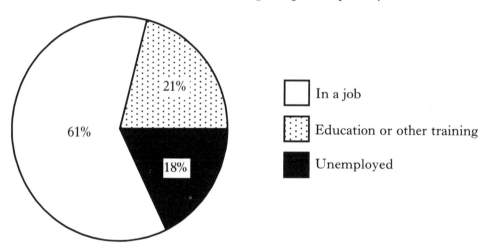

Source D4(b): **Unemployment in Strathglen (figures in 000s)**

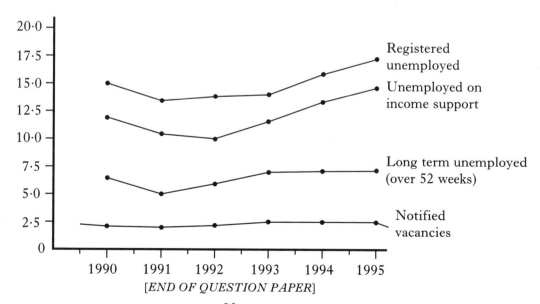

[*END OF QUESTION PAPER*]

SCOTTISH
CERTIFICATE OF
EDUCATION
1997

FRIDAY, 16 MAY
1.00 PM – 3.30 PM

MODERN STUDIES
HIGHER GRADE
Paper II
Decision Making Exercise 2

Attempt:

Either   Decision Making Exercise 1:   Income and Wealth in a Democratic Society;

Or   Decision Making Exercise 2: Health Care in a Democratic Society but **not both**. The Decision Making Exercises are contained in separate booklets.

A summary of the exercise is provided on the cover of each booklet.

Read the summaries carefully before deciding which exercise to attempt.   In each case, answer **all** questions.

DECISION MAKING EXERCISE 2:

HEALTH CARE IN A DEMOCRATIC SOCIETY

Summary of Decision Making Exercise

You are a member of the Board of Directors of the Glenwood Royal Hospital Trust.   You have been asked by the Chairperson of the Trust to prepare a report on possible ways of balancing the Trust's annual budget.

Before beginning the task, you must answer a number of evaluating questions (Questions 1–5) based on the source material provided. The source material is as follows:

        Source A: Efficiency Savings Package

        Source B: Increase Income Package

        Source C: Letter Page

        Source D: Statistical Survey

DECISION MAKING EXERCISE 2

QUESTIONS

Marks

Questions 1 to 5 are based on Sources A to D on pages 2–7. Answer Questions 1 to 5 before attempting Question 6.

In Questions 1 to 5, use <u>only</u> the sources described in each question.

Question 1

*Use **only** Source A and Source D5.*

What evidence is there that the Glenwood Royal Hospital Trust has privatised some of its services since 1981?

2

Question 2

*Use **only** Source B, Source D1 and Source D2.*

To what extent does the evidence support Karen Menzies' claim that the Glenwood Trust could benefit from making use of the Private Finance Initiative?

3

Question 3

*Use **only** Source B, Source C1 and Source C2.*

Contrast the views of Karen Menzies, Sheila Wilson and John Rennie on the effects of the NHS internal market on Trust hospitals.

3

Question 4

*Use **only** Source C1 and Source D3.*

Quote an example of the selective use of facts in Sheila Wilson's letter. Give a reason for **and** against the statement in your answer.

3

Question 5

*Use **only** Source A, Source C2 and Source D4.*

Compare the views of Bill Cuthbert and John Rennie on bed capacity in Glenwood Trust. Give a reason to support **each** view.

4

(15)

Question 6

DECISION MAKING TASK

You are a member of the Board of Directors of the Glenwood Royal Hospital Trust. You have been asked by the Chairperson of the Trust to prepare a report on possible ways of balancing the Trust's annual budget.

In your report you should:

* recommend a package which will save money **either** through increased efficiency **or** by earning income for the Trust;

* provide arguments to support your package;

* give reasons for rejecting the other package, including any political and social arguments which may be presented by those who oppose your recommendation.

In your report you **must** use:

* the **source material** provided and

* other **background knowledge**.

Your answer should be written in a style appropriate to a *report*.

The written and statistical information sources which have been provided are as follows:

SOURCE A: Efficiency Savings Package

SOURCE B: Increase Income Package

SOURCE C: Letter Page

SOURCE D: Statistical Survey

(35)

Total 50 Marks

SOURCE A: EFFICIENCY SAVINGS PACKAGE

At the recent emergency meeting of Glenwood Royal Hospital Trust, it emerged that the Trust's annual budget had been overspent by £5 million. As requested, the package I have prepared for your consideration involves the introduction of a series of efficiency savings which will help to get the Trust
5   out of debt.

While it is important to keep some beds free for emergencies, empty beds are a serious drain on the Trust's resources. One obvious way to make savings, therefore, would be to reduce the number of the Trust's spare beds. There are different ways in which this could be achieved. For example, with
10   improvements in technology and medication, it is now possible to perform many surgical operations on a day-care basis with patients being able to return home in the evening. Also, with careful planning, it would be possible to arrange for more serious surgical operations to be performed early in the week, thereby allowing the majority of patients to be discharged by Friday. In doing
15   this, complete wards could be closed down over the weekend, saving substantially on wage bills and heating costs. Finally, making some wards mixed male/female would give management more flexibility, freeing even more beds for other uses.

The main focus of this plan is the delivery of a quality service to meet the
20   current and future needs of patients. It is important to maintain a level of nursing staff capable of achieving this. It is evident, however, that wage bills for nurses are the largest expenditure for the Trust. Given the financial crisis in which the Trust now finds itself, the number of nurses should be adjusted accordingly. Costs could be cut, for example, by not making new
25   appointments to fill vacant promoted posts, by putting more nurses on short term contracts and by employing a higher proportion of less expensive health care assistants to carry out routine nursing jobs. In addition, while the Trust should honour its duty by paying nurses the nationally agreed part of their pay rise, it should not, on this occasion, pay the additional local reward.

30   For a number of years the Glenwood Trust has been putting out to competitive tender its ancillary services such as catering, cleaning and laundry. This has helped to produce substantial savings for the Trust, and the Trust should now be considering a wider range of services, such as kidney dialysis and intensive care unit nursing, for competitive tendering.

Bill Cuthbert (Brydon & Co, Management Consultants)

SOURCE B: INCREASE INCOME PACKAGE

As instructed, a package of measures to meet the financial needs of Glenwood Royal Hospital Trust has been prepared for your consideration. If this package is implemented, it will earn sufficient new income to wipe out the Trust's debt.

5   The creation of the internal market has meant that the more services NHS Trusts can sell, the more money they can earn. Instead of cutting services, therefore, Glenwood Trust should be looking at ways of raising productivity as a way out of this financial crisis. The Trust could, for example, increase the number of patient treatments performed by encouraging its doctors to
10   perform more operations, and to discharge patients as soon as possible. Increasing productivity in this way would, of course, reduce waiting lists.

The Trust can generate new income by developing partnerships with the private sector. Links should be made with the two large private hospitals providing acute care close to the Trust. There are also insurance companies
15   who would be prepared to work in partnership with the Trust to provide a better quality of care for their customers—as well as increasing their own profits. The Trust should inform these private companies that its expensive medical equipment is available for hire when not in use by the staff of Glenwood Royal Hospital. In future, the Trust should also consider shared
20   ownership of new, high technology equipment. This arrangement would enable both NHS and private patients to benefit from the most advanced technology. Indeed, there is no reason why the Trust should not consider hiring out one of its operating theatres to the private medical companies.

The Private Finance Initiative, introduced by the Conservative Government
25   in 1992, aims at persuading the private sector to finance, build and even manage new NHS hospitals or departments. Moreover, Trusts are now able to borrow as much as £10 million from the private sector without Treasury approval. Glenwood Trust should raise money from this source in order to build a new wing devoted to increasing the number of pay beds within the
30   hospital. After all, the huge rise in people covered by private health insurance in recent years means that this could become a significant source of income for the Trust.

Karen Menzies (Business First, Management Consultants)

SOURCE C: LETTER PAGE

C1

SIR: People must stop giving out the message that the NHS in general, and the Glenwood Trust in particular, is in a state of crisis.   The truth of the matter is that the reverse is the case.

5 We have to accept that the market system introduced by the NHS reforms has completely changed the financial basis on which hospitals are run.   Unlike hospitals in the old NHS, Trusts are commercial enterprises which have to put the interest of their customers first.   Trusts have responded to the laws of the market by increasing their efficiency and the quality of their services.   At Glenwood, for example, the standard of patient care, in all categories, now compares favourably with that offered 10 by other providers.

It is also important that the so-called "crisis" at Glenwood is put into perspective. The £5 million shortfall is less than 2% of the Trust's total annual budget.   There is no reason, therefore, why an efficiency savings programme should harm patient care at all.

Sheila Wilson

C2

SIR: It is now quite clear that the NHS reforms have not had the positive effects we were promised.   The present crisis at Glenwood Trust must convince even the most ardent supporters of the reforms that one of their effects is that Trust hospitals are now no different from any other commercial enterprise which may run out of money 5 and be forced to close down.

Even if it does not come to that, however, the internal market has failed, most certainly, to put standards up.   There is a very obvious shortage of acute spare beds available in Glenwood, as is proven by the number of patients awaiting treatment and, indeed, it is getting increasingly difficult to find any throughout the country.   A 10 bout of severe weather would reveal the real extent of these shortages.   Where would those patients with chest infections, injuries from accidents caused by icy pavements or roads, and victims of hypothermia be treated?   Glenwood Royal Hospital would be unable to cope.

John Rennie

SOURCE D: STATISTICAL SURVEY

Source D1:   Map of Glenwood area

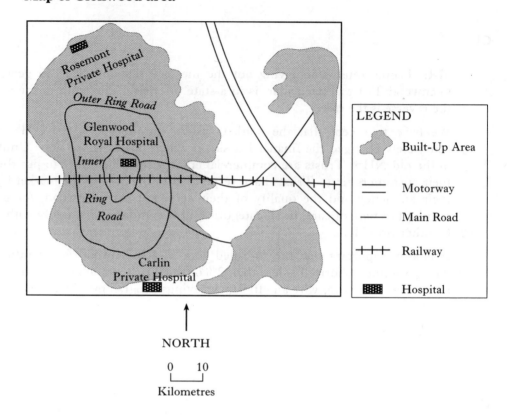

Source D2:   Private Medical Insurance

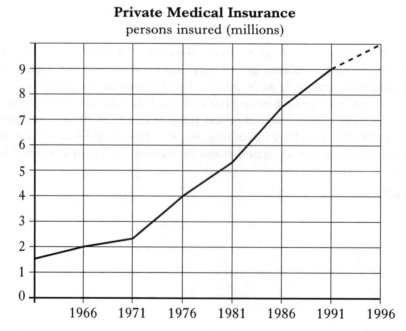

Source: Adapted from Lee Donaldson Associates, BUPA, Dept of Health

Source D3:   **Hospital Performance 1996–97**

Hospital	Category (in %)					
	A	**B**	**C**	**D**	**E**	**F**
All Providers	75·8	80·9	97·8	2·0	45·2	80·8
Glenwood NHS Trust	70·6	78·9	98·0	2·3	40·2	80·3

In the table the figures refer to:

A New outpatients—% given appointment within 9 weeks of referral

B % inpatients and day cases treated within 3 months of being on waiting list

C % inpatients and day cases treated within 12 months of being on waiting list

D % of planned admissions cancelled by the hospital

E Day cases as a % of all admissions to the hospital

F % of complaints dealt with within 4 weeks.

Source D4:   **Residents within the area serviced by Glenwood Royal Hospital awaiting treatment**

April 1996–March 1997						
	Time in Months					
Day Cases	0–3		3–12		12–18	
	Number	%	Number	%	Number	%
Cardiology	95	96	4	4		
General Surgery	517	65	273	35	3	0·4
Gynaecology	113	93	8	7		
Oral Surgery/Oral Medicine	77	48	72	45	12	7
Orthopaedic Surgery	121	62	70	36	4	2
Plastic Surgery	147	23	335	53	156	24

Source: Information Services Division

Source D5:   Changes in NHS Workforce in the UK 1981 and 1992

	1981	1992	Difference	% Change
Medical & Dental	49,700	58,800	+9,100	+18·3
Nursing & Midwifery	492,800	484,500	−8,300	−1·7
Professional & Technical	80,200	110,800	+30,600	+38·2
Administrative & Clerical	133,300	187,000	+53,700	+40·3
Ancillary	220,100	106,100	−114,000	−51·8
Other non-medical	56,200	53,400	−2,800	−5·0
Total	1,032,300	1,000,600		

Source: Pulse Publications: Politics of Health
Adapted from *Social Trends 24*, OPCS 1994, 7.40

[END OF QUESTION PAPER]

SCOTTISH
CERTIFICATE OF
EDUCATION
1998

WEDNESDAY, 20 MAY
9.30 AM – 12.00 NOON

MODERN STUDIES
HIGHER GRADE
Paper I

SECTION A—Politics in a Democratic Society (Study Theme 1)

Answer ONE question from this Section

Marks

Question A1

(a) Describe the internal organisation of the Conservative Party. **10**

(b) Discuss the aims of Labour Party policy on **two** of the following:

Employment;

Health;

Taxation. **15**

(25)

Question A2

Study Reference Table QA2 and answer the questions which follow.

Reference Table QA2 : Conservative, Labour and Liberal Democrat* General Election Performance 1983–1997

	1983		1992		1997	
	Seats	% vote	Seats	% vote	Seats	% vote
Conservative	397	42	336	41·9	165	31·4
Labour	209	27·6	271	34·4	419	44·4
Liberal Democrat * Alliance (1983)	23	25·4	20	17·8	46	17·3

(a) Discuss the advantages and disadvantages of the UK electoral system. **13**

(b) Describe the possible **disadvantages** of changing to a system of proportional representation (PR). (In your answer you should refer to different systems of PR.) **12**

(25)

Question A3

(a) Describe, using examples, the different types of pressure groups in the UK. **5**

(b) To what extent is pressure group activity a threat to democracy? **10**

(c) In what ways does the media influence political opinion? **10**

(25)

Question A4

(a) *In recent years, members of the House of Commons have failed to maintain the highest standards of **parliamentary** behaviour expected of them.*

Discuss. **10**

(b) Describe those factors which contribute to the power of the Prime Minister. **15**

(25)

Marks

Question A5

(a) Describe the role of **each** of the following in political decision-making for Scotland:

The Scottish Office;

Scottish Question Time;

The Scottish Grand Committee.

12

(b) Examine the Government's plans for **both** election to, and the powers of, a devolved Scottish parliament.

13

(25)

Question A6

(a) Outline the main services provided by local authorities.

5

(b) To what extent does Central Government control local authority finance?

10

(c) What are the arguments **both** for and against full-time, paid councillors?

10

(25)

**SECTION B—Income and Wealth in a Democratic Society (Study Theme 2),
Health Care in a Democratic Society (Study Theme 3)**

Answer ONE question from this Section

Marks

Question B7

  (a) Describe the ways in which social class can be defined.   **10**

  (b) What reasons may there be for growing income inequality between the rich and the poor in
the UK?   **15**

        (25)

Question B8

  (a) Examine the economic and social problems faced by the unemployed in the UK.   **12**

  (b) Describe government policies aimed at reducing the number of people receiving benefits.   **13**

        (25)

Question B9

  (a) To what extent do women in the UK experience economic and social disadvantage?   **10**

  (b) Describe the attempts made in recent years to achieve political, economic and social equality
for women.   **15**

        (25)

Question B10

  (a) *Changes in primary health care plus the growth in the private sector have led to the
criticism that the UK has a two-tier health service.*

     Discuss.   **12**

  (b) Why is the NHS struggling to meet its original aims?   **13**

        (25)

Question B11

  (a) Describe the main features of community care.   **12**

  (b) Examine the criticisms of the way community care has worked in practice.   **13**

        (25)

Question B12

  (a) Examine the main features of the internal market in health care.   **12**

  (b) In what ways has there been an increase in **both** patient rights and choice in health care?   **13**

        (25)

SECTION C—International Issues

Answer TWO questions from this Section

Please note that within each Study Theme a choice is provided.

Answer only ONE question in relation to a single Study Theme.

REGIONAL AND NATIONAL CONFLICT (STUDY THEME 4)

Marks

Question C13

EITHER A   South Africa

A.   *Faced with very serious housing shortages, rising unemployment, an unstoppable crime rate and a shortage of schools, South Africa's black majority is growing impatient as it waits for promised improvements from the ANC leadership.*

     (*a*)   What evidence is there that South Africa faces a number of social and economic problems?   **10**

     (*b*)   In what ways has the ANC attempted to solve these problems?   **9**

     (*c*)   To what extent is there a political opposition to the ANC?   **6**

           (25)

OR B   Arab-Israeli Conflict

B.   (*a*)   Describe the role of the USA and other members of the international community in the Arab-Israeli peace process.   **13**

     (*b*)   To what extent are there still obstacles to permanent peace?   **12**

           (25)

MINORITIES (STUDY THEME 5)

Question C14

EITHER A   National and Religious Minorities in the Soviet Union and its Successor States

A.   (*a*)   Describe the problems faced by Russians in the successor states of the USSR.   **10**

     (*b*)   What evidence has there been of expressions of **both** religious and national identity in the successor states? **(You should refer to at least two states in your answer.)**   **15**

           (25)

OR B   Ethnic Minorities in the USA

B.   (*a*)   To what extent **and** with what success do ethnic minorities participate in politics?   **10**

     (*b*)   What evidence is there that ethnic minority groups continue to experience social and economic disadvantage?   **15**

           (25)

INTERNATIONAL COOPERATION AND CONFLICT (STUDY THEME 6)

Marks

Question C15

EITHER A The European Union

A. (a) What are the **main** obstacles to closer political and economic cooperation between members of the European Union? **15**

(b) To what extent has the Common Agricultural Policy been reformed in recent years? **10**

(25)

OR B The United Nations

B. (a) What part does **each** of the following play in achieving the aims of the UNO?

General Assembly

Security Council

General Secretary **13**

(b) *The UN's reputation has suffered since the early 1990s because it has failed to achieve peace in major armed conflicts.*

Discuss. **12**

(25)

IDEOLOGY AND DEVELOPMENT (STUDY THEME 7)

Question C16

EITHER A The USA

A. (a) Examine the role of "downsizing" in the US economy. **10**

(b) In what ways does the Federal Government attempt to reduce poverty for **both** the employed and unemployed? **15**

(25)

OR B Russia

B. (a) To what extent has Russia become a market economy? **12**

(b) In what ways has Russia become more democratic? **13**

(25)

OR C China

C. (a) To what extent has China become a market economy? **12**

(b) In what ways do the Chinese authorities limit social and political freedom? **13**

(25)

POLITICS OF THE ENVIRONMENT (STUDY THEME 8)

Question C17   *Marks*

   EITHER A   The Politics of Energy

A.   (*a*)   Describe the British Government's energy policy.   **10**

   (*b*)   Examine the arguments **against** the continued use of nuclear energy.   **15**

                                                                                     (25)

OR B   The Politics of Food

B.   **With reference to either North East Africa (excluding Egypt) or Southern Africa, answer the questions below.**

   (*a*)   Describe the social and political factors which make the production and distribution of food difficult.   **13**

   (*b*)   Examine the role of the UN specialised agencies in dealing with food shortages.   **12**

                                                                                     (25)

[END OF QUESTION PAPER]

SCOTTISH
CERTIFICATE OF
EDUCATION
1998

WEDNESDAY, 20 MAY
1.00 PM – 3.30 PM

MODERN STUDIES
HIGHER GRADE
Paper II
Decision Making Exercise 1

Attempt:

Either   Decision Making Exercise 1: Income and Wealth in a Democratic Society;

Or   Decision Making Exercise 2: Health Care in a Democratic Society but **not both**. The Decision Making Exercises are contained in separate booklets.

A summary of the exercise is provided on the cover of each booklet.

Read the summaries carefully before deciding which exercise to attempt. In each case, answer **all** questions.

DECISION MAKING EXERCISE 1 :

INCOME AND WEALTH IN A DEMOCRATIC SOCIETY

Summary of Decision Making Exercise

You are a policy researcher for a university. You have been asked to prepare a report for the employers' organisation, the Confederation of British Industry (CBI), in which you have to recommend or reject the trades unions' proposal for a minimum wage of £4·00 an hour for all employees in the UK.

Before beginning the task, you must answer a number of evaluating questions (Questions 1–5) based on the source material provided. The source material is as follows:

        SOURCE A: Statement by trade union spokesperson

        SOURCE B: Statement by Glasgow businessman

        SOURCE C: Viewpoints

        SOURCE D: Statistical Survey

DECISION MAKING EXERCISE 1

QUESTIONS

Marks

Questions 1 to 5 are based on Sources A to D on pages 2–7. Answer Questions 1 to 5 before attempting Question 6.

In Questions 1 to 5, use <u>only</u> the sources described in each question.

Question 1

Use **only** *Source A and Source B.*

In what ways do the views of Bob Robertson and Jim Lloyd differ on the effects of a legal minimum wage on jobs?

2

Question 2

(a) *Use* **only** *Source D2 and Source A.*

Give evidence to support the view of Bob Robertson on low pay.

2

(b) *Use* **only** *Source D3 and Source B.*

Give evidence to support Jim Lloyd's claim about low earners in the area in which he lives.

2

Question 3

Use **only** *Source A, Source B and Source D1.*

What evidence is there to support the views of both Bob Robertson and Jim Lloyd on the effects of a minimum wage on unemployment?

4

Question 4

Use **only** *Source C2, Source D4 and Source D5.*

For what reasons might Tricia Pentland be accused of exaggeration?

3

Question 5

Use **only** *Source C1 and Source D6.*

In what way does the evidence support Moira McLean's claim on the effects of the minimum wage on her company's wage bill?

2

(15)

Question 6

DECISION MAKING TASK

You are a policy researcher for a university. You have been asked to prepare a report for the employers' organisation, the Confederation of British Industry (CBI), in which you have to recommend or reject the trades unions' proposal for a minimum wage of £4·00 an hour for all employees in the UK.

In your report you should:

* recommend or reject the trades unions' proposal of a national minimum wage of £4·00 an hour for all employees in the UK;

* provide arguments to support your recommendation;

* describe any difficulties or cost implications which might follow from your recommendations.

In your report you **must** use:

* the **source material** provided and

* other **background knowledge**.

Your answer should be written in a style appropriate to a *report*.

The written and statistical information sources which have been provided are as follows:

SOURCE A: Statement by trade union spokesperson

SOURCE B: Statement by Glasgow businessman

SOURCE C: Viewpoints

SOURCE D: Statistical Survey

(35)

Total: 50 Marks

SOURCE A: STATEMENT BY TRADE UNION SPOKESPERSON

There is an overwhelming case for a national minimum wage. In the UK, 1 in 3 children is being brought up in poverty. As recent evidence shows, not only does 25% of the country earn less than the national average, there is a growing gap between the rich and the poor. Our members have been told for years that
5   inequality is no bad thing; that as the rich get richer their wealth "trickles down" to the poor. This is not so. A report from Dr Richard Reading from Norwich shows that 2000 children die in the UK each year because they are poor. It is one of the strongest arguments yet for a national minimum wage.

Britain has become the "sweatshop of Europe". We are the only EU country
10   not to have a national minimum wage. How arrogant for us to believe that our economic policies are right and all our European partners are wrong. The scandal of low pay affects all workers but, despite Government legislation, vulnerable groups of people, especially women, are particularly affected. The Council of Europe estimates that a decent wage would be £6·03 an hour. All
15   we are asking for is a national minimum wage of £4 an hour. This is not excessive but it would take thousands of workers out of the poverty trap.

Tight-fisted employers will complain that they "cannot afford" to pay more. They cannot afford not to! A minimum wage of £4 an hour would be good for business. Poorly paid workers are poorly motivated, do poor quality work and
20   are more likely to quit the job. A survey carried out by the Reed Personnel Services Employment agency in 1996 found that 49% of the employers who responded were in favour of a minimum wage.

A minimum wage will not cost jobs! The experience in the USA has shown that when the minimum wage was increased there was little effect on job
25   losses. If paying workers decent wages was bad for the economy, the USA would suffer from higher unemployment than we do. With decent wages available for all we can break the poverty trap. As people get back to work the whole country benefits, with less to pay out on Jobseeker's Allowance and the government receives more in tax and national insurance receipts.

30   The extent of poverty in Britain is a national disgrace. That is why we need a national minimum wage of £4 an hour now!

Bob Robertson

SOURCE B: STATEMENT BY GLASGOW BUSINESSMAN

A national minimum wage will be a disaster for the British economy. Our low unemployment is the envy of our European partners. The bad old days of unions running the country are gone. Our workers are flexible and reasonable in their wage demands and, as a result, wages for those in work are higher than
5   ever. We are all in favour of a high wage economy, but to enforce it by law, when companies cannot afford it, is economic madness. Now that Britain has moved out of recession, misguided demands from unions threaten our prosperity. Our estimates show that a minimum wage will destroy about 1·7 million jobs because not all businesses can afford to pay at least £4 an hour
10 to every employee. The unions' plans would replace low pay with no pay.

Those countries that have a national minimum wage have a higher level of unemployment than we do. In the area in which I live, most low earners are not full-time employees but are teenagers or women seeking some extra cash for holidays. Many companies could not afford to pay every paperboy and girl
15 and every supermarket shelf stacker £4 an hour. The result would be fewer teenagers being able to take up part-time work and, therefore, stay on at school or take a college course.

A minimum wage would increase prices as employers pass on wage rises to their customers. Inflation will get worse. How are British firms supposed to
20 compete with German, Japanese and American companies with this burden placed on them? At the end of the day the effect would be the same—major companies would close down or move to other countries where wages are lower. In the age of the Internet, individual workers in the new global economy need to be flexible. Higher pay has to be earned through higher
25 profits and the best workers will be the best paid.

The key to economic success is to have businesses selling their products in the international market and creating well paid jobs.

                                                                    Jim Lloyd

SOURCE C: VIEWPOINTS

Source C1:   Moira McLean, Managing Director of Lloyds & Son

The vast majority of employers are desperately worried about this minimum wage proposal. Our wage costs for all workers would go up, leaving us with no option but to employ fewer people. We employ 17,000 staff across the UK. If the minimum wage of £4 becomes law, we would have to increase the pay of
5   the majority of our workers. It is more than likely that our professional staff would demand an increase too, as they would not wish to see their wages slipping in relation to unskilled, part-time workers.

We pay a minimum wage of £2·50 an hour, as well as providing full training and live-in accommodation. Most of our staff are under 25 and come from
10   regions of the country which have some of the highest rates of unemployment. Paying everyone higher wages sounds the right thing to do, but no company, in any industry, can afford to pay £4 an hour. To pay for it we would have to cut back on customer services and entertainment, which, in the tourist sector, the fastest growing in the British economy, would be a disaster.

Source C2:   Tricia Pentland, low paid worker

My life would be transformed by a minimum wage of £4 an hour. Just now I earn £2·85 an hour, working in the local supermarket. I am a single parent and I have my 5 year old son to look after. This prevents me from working more hours. With the unions' plans I would earn around £50 a week more
5   and I could afford to take my son on holiday and have little treats.

Low pay isn't just a problem in my so-called "woman's job". All workers are seeing their wages being cut and their standards of living lowered so that they cannot even afford to go on holiday. The pay is so low in many jobs you are better off on benefits. A minimum wage will allow people to get out of the
10   benefit trap and become independent. The "haves" are earning more and the "have nots" are getting poorer. It disgusts me to read of these "fat cat" directors earning huge salaries. They earn more in an afternoon than I do all month!

SOURCE D: **STATISTICAL SURVEY**

Source D1: **Unemployment Rates (%) 1996**
Countries with a national minimum wage (except UK)

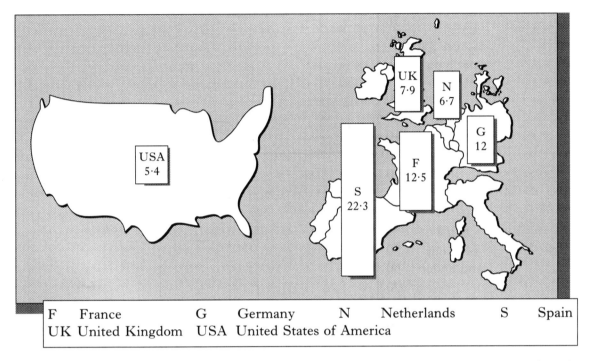

| F | France | G | Germany | N | Netherlands | S | Spain |
| UK | United Kingdom | USA | United States of America | | | | |

Source: Low Pay Unit (adapted)

Source D2: **Numbers of people in the UK earning under £4 an hour**

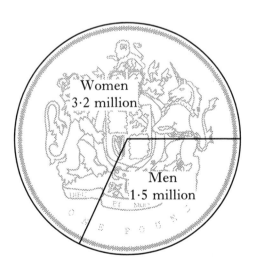

Source: Low Pay Unit/Labour Force Survey, 1995 (adapted)

Source D3: **Gross hourly pay of employees in the Greater Glasgow area**

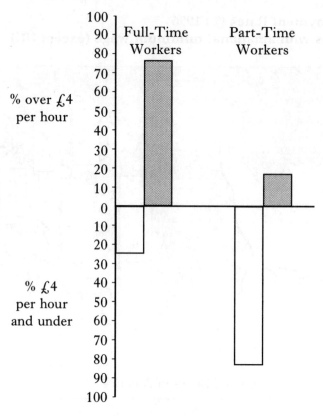

Source: Low Pay Unit/Labour Force Survey, 1995 (adapted)

Source D4: **Average gross weekly pay for all UK full-time employees**

	Women	Men
1994	£244·41	£335·60
1993	£237·40	£333·00
1992	£221·90	£324·60
1991	£206·50	£299·50

Source: New Earnings Survey, 1994 (adapted)

Source D5:   Holidays taken by UK residents

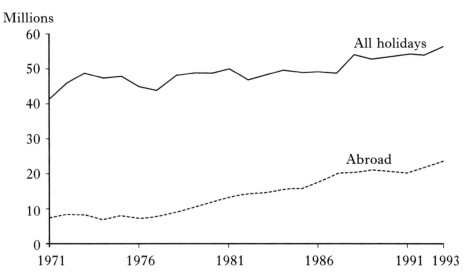

Source: *Social Trends,* 1995

Source D6:   Workforce of Lloyds & Son, 1996—percentage of workforce in each wage category

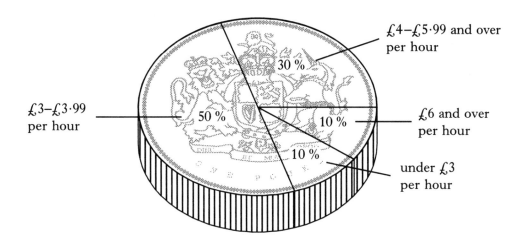

[END OF QUESTION PAPER]

SCOTTISH
CERTIFICATE OF
EDUCATION
1998

WEDNESDAY, 20 MAY
1.00 PM – 3.30 PM

MODERN STUDIES
HIGHER GRADE
Paper II
Decision Making Exercise 2

Attempt:

Either Decision Making Exercise 1: Income and Wealth in a Democratic Society;

Or Decision Making Exercise 2: Health Care in a Democratic Society but **not both**. The Decision Making Exercises are contained in separate booklets.

A summary of the exercise is provided on the cover of each booklet.

Read the summaries carefully before deciding which exercise to attempt. In each case, answer **all** questions.

DECISION MAKING EXERCISE 2:

HEALTH CARE IN A DEMOCRATIC SOCIETY

Summary of Decision Making Exercise

You are a Health Policy Researcher. Prepare a report for Strathkeith Council recommending whether or not £90,000 should be allocated to setting up a "Men's Health Project" in the Strathkeith area.

Before beginning the task, you must answer a number of evaluating questions (Questions 1–4) based on the source material provided. The source material is as follows:

Source A: Statement by spokesperson for the Men's Health Project

Source B: Extract from speech by Councillor Hutchison

Source C: Viewpoints

Source D: Statistical Survey

DECISION MAKING EXERCISE 2

QUESTIONS

Marks

Questions 1 to 4 are based on Sources A to D on pages 2–6.   Answer Questions 1 to 4 before attempting Question 5.

In Questions 1 to 4, use <u>only</u> the sources described in each question.

Question 1

Use Source A and Source B.

In what ways do the views of the spokesperson for the Men's Health Project and Councillor Hutchison differ on the factors contributing to poor health?

2

Question 2

Use Source B, Source D1 and Source D4.

In what ways does the evidence support Councillor Hutchison's view on men's use of their GPs?

2

Question 3

(*a*)   *Use Source C1, Source D3 and Source D4.*

What is the view expressed by Gavin Berstan on the level of funding for the NHS in Scotland and its consequences for the nation's health?

To what extent does the evidence support this view?

3

(*b*)   *Use Source C2 and Source D4.*

To what extent has Mairi Hamilton been selective in her use of the facts with regard to cancer and heart disease?

3

Question 4

(*a*)   *Use Source A and Source D2.*

To what extent might the spokesperson for the Men's Health Project be accused of exaggeration?

3

(*b*)   *Use Source C1 and Source C2.*

In what ways do the views of Gavin Berstan and Mairi Hamilton differ on the usefulness of the Men's Health Project in improving health in Strathkeith?

2

(15)

Question 5

DECISION MAKING TASK

You are a Health Policy Researcher. Prepare a report for Strathkeith Council recommending whether or not £90,000 should be allocated to setting up a "Men's Health Project" in the Strathkeith area.

In your report you should:

* recommend whether or not the project should go ahead;

* provide arguments to support your recommendation;

* identify and comment on any arguments which may be presented by those who oppose your recommendation.

In your report you **must** use:

* the **source material** provided and

* other **background knowledge**.

Your answer should be written in a style appropriate to a *report*.

The written and statistical information sources which have been provided are as follows:

SOURCE A: Statement by spokesperson for the Men's Health Project

SOURCE B: Extract from speech by Councillor Hutchison

SOURCE C: Viewpoints

SOURCE D: Statistical Survey

(35)

Total 50 Marks

SOURCE A: STATEMENT BY SPOKESPERSON FOR THE MEN'S HEALTH PROJECT

It has long been recognised that Scottish men suffer from some of the worst health in Britain. Indeed, Scotland is often referred to as "the sick man of Europe". It is now widely accepted that unemployment and poor housing conditions are contributory factors to the high rates of cancer, heart disease,
5   depression and suicide, especially among men.

The British Medical Association (BMA) has reported that the number of people suffering heart attacks in the 24–64 age range in an area of multiple deprivation increases with both age and the degree of deprivation. After a heart attack, those from more deprived areas are more likely to die than those
10   who come from more affluent areas. A recently published medical journal has argued that when allocating resources to tackle heart disease, social class differences should be taken into account.

There is also a gender division in death rates. Women have a longer life expectancy than men. Illnesses such as cancer and heart disease affect men
15   more than women. These are conditions which medical experts say could be significantly reduced by encouraging positive action towards healthier living— one of the main objectives of the Men's Health Project.

The establishment of the Men's Health Project will help to combat some of these problems. It is well-known that men are more reluctant to visit their
20   GPs. They often put off any consultation until the onset of really serious symptoms and, therefore, expensive treatment is needed. The Health Project would provide an opportunity for men to meet and discuss the health issues which affect them. They would receive advice on diet, exercise and coping with stress, as well as support for cutting down on smoking and alcohol.

25   The £90,000 needed to start the project would be money well-spent. There are always competing demands for council funds, but the Men's Health Project would provide positive social benefits to an area in which large sections of the population experience multiple deprivation. It would appear that there is always an emphasis on women's health. It is now time to even out this
30   disparity. There is no doubt that men's health is worse than women's health and this should be recognised by council's funding of this project.

SOURCE B: EXTRACT FROM SPEECH BY COUNCILLOR HUTCHISON

The proposed Men's Health Project would be an unjustifiable waste of money. We do not need this because the nation's health is improving anyway. Both local and central government have spent money on positive health campaigns. Our own council has spent money on a campaign to persuade
5   children to eat a more healthy diet.

There are other ways in which this money could be better spent. People should take responsibility for their own health and not expect somebody else to do it for them. What society needs now is more individual responsibility and less of the "nanny state". It is well-known that smoking, excess alcohol,
10   poor diet and lack of proper exercise are bad for health. It does not take £90,000 to point this out. Yes, people in Scotland smoke too much. Yes, people in Scotland drink too much—the level of alcohol consumption in Scotland is far too high and is certainly worse than anywhere else in Britain. However, I strongly object to wasting money on telling people what they
15   already know. The Government is already spending taxpayers' money in this way.

To argue that men's health problems in Strathkeith are caused by unemployment and social deprivation is politically-motivated nonsense which ignores the facts. Scotland's unemployment rate is far lower than the rest of
20   the UK and housing conditions are no worse than in any other part of the country.

It is nonsense to suggest that men suffer more ill-health than women! Statistics clearly show that women have more severe health problems than men. There is certainly no justification for spending any more money on
25   additional health facilities for men. If men have any health problems, all they need to do is visit their GP or attend one of the clinics offered within the GP's practice. It is perfectly clear than men do not make full use of these facilities. This is highlighted by the higher death rates in men from conditions which may be treated, if diagnosed sooner rather than later.

SOURCE C: VIEWPOINTS

C1

Poor health is a serious problem in this country and much of it has social and economic causes. A Men's Health Project in Strathkeith would be a good idea and would go some way to reducing the effects of the multiple deprivation which exists in this area. Projects like these are not the real solution to this country's health
5 problems. Scotland has continued to be the poor relation with regard to health care spending and, if Strathkeith is a good example, has suffered a greater degree of ill-health.

There is no doubt that we are failing to achieve the aims of the NHS. The nation's health should not be a local issue, it is the nation's problem. It is Central
10 Government, not Local Government which should be addressing the problem.

Gavin Berstan

C2

Money spent on a Men's Health Project would not be money well-spent. Statistics clearly show that health is improving for all groups of people in society—men and women alike, and in all social classes. In particular, the treatment of heart disease and cancer in both men and women has been a great success.

5 Health spending has been increasing in real terms every year. More people are being cured of more illnesses than ever before. More money is being spent informing people on ways to prevent ill-health. Positive health campaigns have been a continued success. People are now better informed on health issues than ever before. It is up to the individual to make use of that information and make the
10 correct choices for themselves. One more health clinic, repeating the message and duplicating resources which already exist, will make little difference and be a waste of money.

Mairi Hamilton

SOURCE D: STATISTICAL SURVEY

Table D1: Strathkeith—Average number of visits to GP per year per patient

	1993		1994	
Age Range	Male	Female	Male	Female
16–44	4	6	3	5
45–64	5	6	4	6
65–74	6	6	5	6
75+	7	7	5	6

Table D2: Strathkeith—Percentage of males and females reporting sickness

	Long-standing illness		Limiting long-standing illness		Restricted activity in previous 14 days	
	Male	Female	Male	Female	Male	Female
1985	29	31	16	18	11	14
1989	31	33	17	19	11	15
1991	31	32	17	18	11	13
1993	34	35	19	22	13	15
1994	32	32	18	20	12	15
1995	31	31	18	20	13	15

Table D3: Government Expenditure on the National Health Service

	SCOTLAND		UK	
	£ billion	£ per head	£ billion	£ per head
1991/92	3·34	652	31·8	547
1992/93	3·66	715	35·4	609
1993/94	3·78	738	37·3	642
1994/95	3·96	773	39·9	687
1995/96	4·11	803	40·7	701

Source: Adapted from Government Expenditure Plans, 1995/6–1996/7 (Scottish Office)
and Public Finance Trends, 1996 (Office for National Statistics)

**Table D4: Scottish death rates by selected cause per 100,000 population
UK average in brackets**

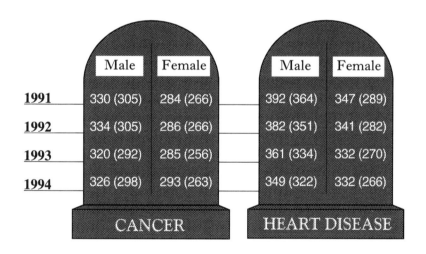

	Male	Female		Male	Female
1991	330 (305)	284 (266)		392 (364)	347 (289)
1992	334 (305)	286 (266)		382 (351)	341 (282)
1993	320 (292)	285 (256)		361 (334)	332 (270)
1994	326 (298)	293 (263)		349 (322)	332 (266)
	CANCER			**HEART DISEASE**	

Source: Adapted from *Regional Trends,* 1993–96

[END OF QUESTION PAPER]

NOTES

NOTES

Printed by Bell & Bain Ltd., Glasgow, Scotland.